D1272059

POLITICS IN THE AGE OF COBDEN

POLITICS IN THE AGE OF COBDEN

John Prest

Fellow of Balliol College, Oxford

First published 1977 by
THE MACMILLAN PRESS LTD
London and Basingstoke
Associated companies in Delhi
Dublin Hong Kong Johannesburg Lagos
Melbourne New York Singapore and Tokyo

Typeset by
SANTYPE INTERNATIONAL LIMITED
(COLDTYPE DIVISION)
Salisbury, Wiltshire

Printed in Great Britain by
BILLING & SONS LTD
Guildford, Worcester and London

British Library Cataloguing in Publication Data

Prest, John
    Politics in the age of Cobden
    1. Great Britain — Politics and government — 1830–1837
    2. Great Britain — Politics and government — 1837–1901
    I. Title
    320.9′41′075   JN216

    ISBN 0-333-22349-7

Contents

Acknowledgements

Only those who have attempted anything of the kind will understand how much I owe to Angela Aitchison for her analysis of the Reform Party in Chapter 4. In addition I want to thank Judy Cooke for living halfway between the British Museum and the newspaper library at Colindale and for her hospitality, Michael Brock and Angus Macintyre for their criticisms of the text, Paul Davies for advice about the law, Don Rickerd for the opportunity to try out much of my material upon scholars in Canada, Mary Bügge for faultless typing, my wife and family for the tact with which they have managed to live with my preoccupations, and my sister Jean for reading the proofs.

I have followed throughout the convention that the adjective formed from the noun Reformer is Liberal.

1 Introduction

In any electoral system it is necessary to have some means of identifying the voters, of enabling those who are qualified to vote to proceed without hindrance to the poll, and of preventing those who are not qualified from doing so. As Macaulay put it in 1841, there had to be some way of letting 'good' voters in and of keeping 'bad' voters out,[1] and the problem was to devise a method that would do both, for every attempt to smooth the path of the genuine elector would make the way easy for the fraudulent voter too, while every check and test intended to eliminate the fraudulent voter would vex and deter the genuine one. And in England, where there were two electoral systems, representing the boroughs and the counties, side by side, and where until 1918 there were many different franchises, the problem was unusually complicated and intractable.

By the end of the seventeenth century the franchises in the English boroughs already were determined by tradition. In a few places residence and the payment of rates conferred the right to vote, and the electorate was large and relatively open. In others the franchise was confined to the owners of certain properties or burgages, to members of the corporation, and to freemen, and in the early eighteenth century the party in power and in possession of the municipal offices was tempted, upon the occasion of a contested and close-run election, to create sufficient freemen to ensure the victory of candidates of its own 'colour'. This was a short-sighted expedient because it diluted the freemen-body and the freemen's charities, and, in order not to antagonise the existing freemen, municipalities increasingly had resort to the manufacture of 'occasional', or temporary, freemen, who survived long enough to vote, and then obligingly yielded up their honours. This was an abuse, and in 1763 an Act was passed, the so-called Durham Act, to prohibit freemen of less than twelve-months standing from proceeding to the poll.[2] This Act seems, in the long run, to have turned the abuse into a new channel: borough oligarchies were compelled to look further ahead, and in 1820–1 the Whig corporation of Nottingham created 491 new 'honorary' burgesses in good time to vote at the next general election (which took place in 1826), while at Leicester the Tories went one better and enrolled no fewer than 800 honorary freemen in two years between 1822 and 1824.[3]

The Durham Act further required the mayor or bailiff of every borough to keep a book in which were to be entered the names of all the citizens, burgesses and freemen entitled to vote at an election for a Member of Parliament. Unfortunately there was no provision made in the Act for the publication of the mayor's book. Consequently some boroughs disregarded the Act and kept no list; some of those which kept lists refused to make them available to Parliamentary candidates of whom they disapproved; and a few actually made changes in the lists before releasing them, or even circulated false ones.[4] That being so, it was left to each borough to solve its electoral problems in its own way. In some of the smaller boroughs, with their tiny constituencies of twelve or fifty persons, there were few problems. The record of the past was conclusive, and a man whose predecessor in the possession of a property had been admitted to the poll was himself entitled to vote. Everybody knew which properties conferred the franchise, and the electors were known to each other, to the non-electors, and to the officials who conducted the poll. There must have been many medium-sized boroughs where similar considerations applied, where men living together in a face-to-face society were acquainted with each other's businesses and each other's rights, and where the returning officer and his assessors had little difficulty in establishing what changes had taken place in the ownership of property through marriage, inheritance and sale, and what changes had taken place among the freemen through coming of age and the service of apprenticeship.

But there were other boroughs, and those not always very large ones, where the increasing mobility of the population and the practice of inviting partisans in neighbouring towns to become honorary freemen, presented an almost insoluble problem; long before the end of the eighteenth century, boroughs of all sizes, headed, apparently, by Lancaster,[5] were plagued by the high proportion of non-resident freemen. In many places these comprised one-quarter or even one-third of the electorate, and in Bristol, where freedom could be claimed by descent through either the male or the female line, they were literally innumerable. Freemen who had left the town and were no longer known and recognised were easily impersonated, and by the early nineteenth century it was an article of faith among the Reformers that at this point the old face-to-face society had broken down.

In the counties, where the forty-shilling freeholders constituted the vast majority of the electorate, landlords had been accustomed, from the time of the Revolution of 1688 at least, in the excitement of a contest, to 'split' their holdings in order to manufacture votes. In such cases the deed of conveyance was a fictitious one; the landlord did not dispose of his property, nothing changed hands or was intended to change hands, and it was tacitly understood that the object was to enable a dependant to vote. One attorney handed the papers to the 'elector' as he mounted the steps on one side of the polling booth: a second received them back as he descended upon the other — hence the name 'snatch-papers'. These proceedings, which were the equivalent of the manufacture of occasional freemen in the boroughs, were declared illegal by an Act of 1696,[6] but in practice it proved difficult to bring prosecutions under this statute, and in an alternative approach to the problem it was enacted in 1711 that no one should be eligible to vote at any election for a knight of the shire who had not been assessed to the land tax and paid the tax.[7] This Act brought the land-tax assessments into the position they were to play, on and off, for over a century, as a check-list of voters, but it was viewed with jealousy by country gentlemen who regarded it as having stood the Revolution on its head. Parliament existed in order to make sure that there was no taxation without representation: henceforward it would be impossible to participate in the representative system unless one had paid one's taxes. The new provision was repealed in 1745, when the pendulum swung one way against the powers of the tax collectors and the central government they represented,[8] and was re-enacted in 1780, when, during the American war, it swung back again.[9]

No man could vote unless he had been assessed to the land tax and paid his tax, but that did not mean that every man who had paid the tax was qualified to vote, and in 1788 a further attempt was made to establish a complete register. In order to reduce the 'Disputes, Delays, Uncertainty and Expense' of elections, an Act was passed, generally known as Stanhope's Act, 'for the better securing of the Rights of Persons qualified to vote at County Elections'.[10] In every county freeholders were to be encouraged to put their names forward to the collector of taxes for inclusion in a register, which, when compiled, would be printed and published by the King's Printer. There were plenty of technical defects in this Act: the obligation imposed upon the freeholder was purely voluntary; the discretion entrusted to the keeper of the register, who was required to accept and enter every claim, was nil; and the problem of sifting and checking claims was met, or rather not met, by the device of giving any person the right to sue in the courts and to recover £20 from an impostor. But these defects could have been remedied in time had there been the will to do so, and, when we find that the Act was first suspended, and then repealed,[11] within a year of its reaching the statute book, it is impossible not to suppose that the real reason was the jealousy still felt universally throughout the English counties towards any extension of the functions of the collectors of taxes and of the centralised machinery of the state.

The first attempts to create an authentic register of voters in both boroughs and counties having failed, the deficiencies of the electoral system continued to be apparent. Whenever party feelings ran high, objections were made to *bona fide* voters, and the two-thirds of the electors whose claims were not in doubt were subjected to delays while the cases of the remaining one-third were heard.[12] Faced with so many problems of adjudication, sheriffs forgot the discretion they possessed as to the choice of the moment to close the poll, and by the early nineteenth century it was not uncommon for the polls to be kept open for fifteen days — the maximum allowed. In the long-drawn-out confusion of a contested election, a moment was almost bound to arrive when the unscrupulous party agent could bring up impostors, who possessed no qualifications whatever, and successfully present them at the booth, while many of the better class of voters, wearied by the effort and perseverance required to prove their claims, departed without voting. Finally, even after the poll had been closed, the dispute was more than likely to be carried upon petition to the House of Commons, where a Select Committee would be appointed to go over the ground again — a process which may ultimately have conditioned some Members to accept that, without trenching upon the privilege of the House to decide disputed elections, it might be advisable to take steps at an earlier stage of the electoral process to ensure that there were fewer of them.

The stimulus to a new attempt to cope with the problem of registration came from an unexpected quarter. In 1797, at the worst moment of the war against the French Revolution, consols fell to forty-seven, and in November Pitt announced that the next year of the war could not be paid for by borrowing. In 1798, in order to augment 'the National Resources at this important Conjuncture', Pitt's administration turned to the land tax, which had hitherto been voted every year since it was introduced (in 1692), for one year at a time. Now, in order, presumably, to soften the blow of his new income tax, Pitt proposed to strike a bargain with parliament and with the taxpayer. In return for an Act making the land tax 'perpetual', Pitt offered the taxpayer the opportunity of 'Redemption and Purchase' — that is to say, he could buy his way out of it.[13] For the government it was a good bargain, for the hour, because it held out the prospect of increased resources immediately. For the taxpayer it was a golden opportunity, in a period of rapidly rising prices, to rid himself of a burden at a cut price. Not surprisingly, then, the redemption proved to be popular, and Act after Act was passed extending the period in which taxpayers might take advantage of this opportunity.

But the Act of 1780 was still in force, making assessment to and payment of the land tax a qualification for a county vote, and the land-tax assessments still served as a check-list of county voters. Accordingly in 1802 it was enacted that a freeholder who redeemed his land tax should not lose his vote.[14] For a time this may have solved the problem, for at first all the returning officer and his assessor had to do at an election was to collate one entry in the book with another. But by 1817 it was recognised that it was almost impossible for these officials to determine questions relating to the lands that were or were not liable to the Land Tax, because the property redeemed had already been so frequently transferred or mixed with other lands.[15] By 1826, when £702,629 worth of assessments had been redeemed and £1,147,305 worth remained outstanding,[16] the land-tax assessment lists had become totally defective as a means of establishing the voters' *bona fide*s, and the introduction of an effective system of registration was becoming urgent.

The diminishing usefulness of the land-tax assessments accentuated all the existing electoral problems. Because much more time had to be spent in hearing objections and examining claims, the average duration of county contests continued to increase towards the permitted maximum. Supporters, kept hanging about in the county town, became involved in scuffles with their rivals, and had to be lodged for days on end at the expense of the candidates. This in turn bore hard upon a landed class, which had borrowed heavily in order to finance the agricultural expansion of the Napoleonic wars, and was now suffering from deflation and reduced prices for agricultural produce (though these were nothing like as low as they would have been had the landowners not been powerful enough to secure the Corn Laws of 1815).[17] The result, Lord Althorp alleged, was to reduce the range of candidates offering themselves for election, and to restrict the representation of the counties to the very wealthy.[18] In all these ways, then, the desire for the creation of an authentic register became linked with the notion of reducing the duration of contests, the violence attendant upon them, and the expenses of elections – the exact form in which it was presented to Parliament in 1831–2.

The problem was reviewed by Select Committees of the House of Commons in 1817 and 1820.[19] Both committees made one recommendation which was ultimately to be regarded as a vital principle of registration law, which was that, in order to allow the majority of voters who had not been challenged to poll uninterruptedly while the claims of the minority who had been challenged were examined, the assessment of claims to vote should be conducted separately from the polling. The suggestion was not taken up, and the tide did not turn until

1826, when the ne> general election took place at a time when many candidates were still embarrassed by the effects of the financial panic of December 1825. Immediately after the meeting of the new Parliament, two more Select Committees were appointed to consider 'the mode of taking the poll' at elections. Lord John Russell took the chair at one, dealing with the boroughs; Lord Althorp at the other, which dealt with the counties. The appointment of these two notable reformers to chair the two committees represented something more than a mere willingness to make adjustments. The want of an effective system of registration, and the fact that even with the existing electorate it took up to fifteen days to complete the poll, had long presented a formidable technical obstacle to a reform of Parliament and an enlargement of the franchise. But MPs themselves, or at any rate those of them who represented constituencies where contested elections were the norm, now had an incentive, as members of a 'club' whose 'subscription' had become too expensive, to overhaul the system. Should they succeed, they would remove one of the barriers to the extended franchises demanded by public opinion. Thus early did the Reform bandwagon begin to roll.

In 1827 Lord John Russell's committee produced a brief report concentrating upon the need to shorten the duration of the polls.[20] Althorp's committee went much further and embodied its proposals in a draft Registration Bill.[21] Opponents alleged that this was a mere copy of the Act of 1788 and would suffer the same fate,[22] but this was not very perceptive. The Act of 1788 had been a tentative one; but what is remarkable about Althorp's committee is the assurance with which it spoke. No longer should the poll be held up by the hearing of disputed cases; no longer should claims and objections be determined in the excited atmosphere of an election. Scrutiny should be separated from passion, and should be carried out not just in another building, as the committees of 1817 and 1820 had envisaged, but at another time. 'That which now took place at the election should in future take place before the election.'[23] To that end it was necessary to establish 'an authentic Register of all persons who have a right to vote for any county', and the register when formed, must be 'a conclusive document . . . no man should have a right to vote, whose name was not registered; and . . . every man whose name was registered should have that right, without further question'.[24] Once the register was in existence it would be possible to divide the counties into electoral districts and to set up a polling booth in each, thus putting an end to the situation in which electors living up to thirty or even forty miles away from the county towns had to make long journeys to the polls. This in turn would reduce the costs of transport (which fell mainly on the candidates) and make it possible to complete the polls in a matter of two or three days. Althorp's committee rose to the level of its task, and spoke with the grandeur of Reform in the ascendant.

For instruments, the committee turned once again to the collectors of taxes, hoping, presumably, that after thirty-nine years the prejudice against them would have diminished. In the details of their Bill they paid attention to the two great weaknesses of the Act of 1788, the failure to cope with persons neglecting to register, and the inadequate provision for the elimination of false entries. The first was to be met by requiring the collectors of taxes to write, twice a year, to every occupier of land, who in turn would be required to furnish the name of his landlord, whose name, if qualified, would then be placed upon the register automatically. The second was to be met by requiring the collectors of taxes to publish a draft list and lay it before the vestry of each parish. Any person, franchised or unenfranchised, would then be able to raise an objection, and twice a year deputies appointed by the sheriff would hear disputed claims and objections. Finally, the Bill provided for a court of appeal from the decisions of the sheriff's deputies, consisting of the sheriff himself assisted by a barrister.

In 1828 a Bill based upon the report of Lord John Russell's committee to limit the duration of the poll in borough elections to six days was introduced by Colonel Davies, who had taken the chair at the committee when Lord John Russell was absent. The Bill passed, after six days had been amended to eight, and henceforward the voters in the boroughs would no longer be able to eat and drink at the candidates' expense for a whole fortnight. Their 'constitutional enjoyment', as Colonel Sibthorp called it, had been curtailed to that extent.[25] Simultaneously, two other Bills were introduced: one, by Lord Althorp, to establish a register of county voters along the lines recommended in the report of his select committee, and the other, by

Lord Nugent, to establish a register of borough voters. Althorp was a persuasive man, while Nugent's arguments, contained in a speech which was perhaps the most able ever made in this cause,[26] were incontrovertible. But both Bills were lost. Why, then, with opinion beginning to run their way, were the Reformers unable to achieve more? In order to answer this question it is necessary to look beyond Althorp's choice of the collectors of taxes as his agents, and vague disquiet lest regular inquiries into the validity of claims would be 'operose',[27] to the fears of men like Lord Lowther.

This gentleman's contribution to English history was that he met the second reading of Althorp's Bill by announcing that, come what may, he would oppose it.[28] He did not articulate his fears, but fortunately Lord Nugent expressed them for him. The truth was that 'the concealment of the numbers of qualifications of those who had a right to vote' meant that the entire electoral process was carried out in a fog in which only a small number of attorneys retained by the dominant interests in both counties and boroughs could find their way about. Lord Nugent might attempt to allay the fears of his opponents by arguing that 'whether gentlemen were inclined to favour the influence of property or the influence of population' they were at present equally crippled, if they wished to stand for Parliament, 'by ignorance'.[29] But both he and Lord Lowther knew that not only would a registration system which worked smoothly remove one of the barriers to the extension of the franchise: the mere publication of an authentic list of voters would reduce the effectiveness of existing methods of social control.

2 The Reform Act of 1832

When Wellington's government fell in November 1830, and the Whigs, led by Earl Grey, came into office, they were committed to a reform of Parliament. The spectacular features of this reform were to be the redistribution of seats and the extension of the franchise, and these are the ones which historians have paid most attention to, but the Reformers were also committed to an improvement in the conduct of elections through the establishment of a register of electors, and Brougham later said that he regarded the system of registration as perhaps the most important part of the constructive clauses of the whole scheme.[1] For this reason the Whigs dealt with redistribution, the extension of the franchise, and the registration of voters all in one Bill. No doubt there was an element of tactical risk in this, for opponents could seek to exploit flaws in the registration system in order to discredit the Bill as a whole, but the risk was counterbalanced by the advantages of steering the registration clauses onto the statute book with the help of the popular breeze in favour of disfranchising Old Sarum and giving representatives to Manchester.

The Reformers were not in a regular majority in the Parliament elected in 1830, but they took a realistic view of the pent-up pressure for Reform, and their original Bill was drafted with an appeal to the country in mind. After the general election of May 1831 they enjoyed a majority in the House of Commons large enough to overwhelm the Conservative opposition there and to do battle with that in the House of Lords. Consequently both the first Bill, introduced in March, and the second and third Bills, introduced in June and December, were large in their scope. One party had come to power at the expense of another, and sought now to consolidate its position. It was not a time for niceties, or for making (more than a few) concessions to those who had themselves refused all concessions for so long. Contemporaries were amazed when they learned of the length of Schedule A (disfranchising the rotten boroughs) and of Schedule B (taking one Member away from each of the smaller ones), and of the government's decision to introduce an uniform household franchise in the boroughs. The Bill discounted old customs and notions, and set aside, injured or extinguished many existing interests. And even if, in the course of the Bill's progress through Parliament, the Cabinet determined not to terminate the franchises of freemen by birth and servitude, that collective electoral abuse, the non-resident freemen, disappeared for ever.

In dealing with the conduct of elections it was decided that, in future, the poll should be limited to two successive days. In the counties sufficient new polling places were to be provided to ensure that no elector had to travel more than fifteen miles to the poll, and in the larger boroughs separate booths were to be constructed and no more than 600 electors were to be assigned to each one. Point after point was settled in a manner which has ever since been accepted as a desirable feature of election practice. And so it was, too, with the registration. The subject involved difficult points of detail, and hitherto the obstructionists had been able to turn these to such good effect that even the Reformers themselves had at times been overawed by them. But the time for timid and tentative essays in registration had passed. Technical problems which could not be resolved to the satisfaction of all parties were to be decided by the will of the party in power. It was not just that the Reformers had the opportunity: they now had no alternative but to make up their own minds upon every point which had perplexed Parliament in 1788—9 and 1828. Every knot that could not be untied must be cut, and it would have to be left to experience and to history to decide whether the Whigs had chosen well.

The Reform Bill was drafted by a committee of four,[2] and the registration section was the work of Sir James Graham, who had been a member of Althorp's Select Committee of 1826—7. Drawing on that experience, Graham determined the basic principles that henceforth claims and objections were to be heard every year, once a year, and that a new register of electors was to be compiled annually. Registration was to be both 'compulsory' and 'sufficient'. Nobody would be allowed to vote whose name was not on the register, and everybody whose name was on the register would be admitted to the poll without any further examination than was involved in asking him to declare, upon oath, that he was the person A.B. named in the register, that he had not already voted at the election, and that he still possessed the property or qualification in respect of which his claim to vote had been admitted.

For instruments the Reformers dropped the unpopular collectors of taxes, forbore to appoint a new breed of permanent registration officials after the Whigs' usual manner of institutional reform, and chose to rely instead upon the familiar overseers of the poor to compile the lists, which would then be 'revised' by barristers, who would also hear all claims and objections.[3] The power of objecting was confined to persons who were themselves electors or had laid claim to be, and in a display of misconceived firmness it was decided that there should be no appeal to the judges from the decisions of the revising barristers, which were to be final — except that, when a contested election led to a petition and the appointment of a Select Committee of the House of Commons to investigate the return, the committee had power, among the privileges of parliament, to amend the register of electors as finalised by the revising barrister. The completed registers were to be placed in the custody of the returning officers in the boroughs and of the clerks of the peace in the counties, who were to have them printed and to make copies available upon request. The costs of the operation were to be split three ways: the expenses of the overseers were to be met out of the poor rate, those of the returning officers and the clerks of the peace out of borough or county funds, while the revising barristers' fees (five guineas a day) were to be paid by the state.

Althorp thought that of all the objections to the various parts of the Reform Bill 'the arguments used against registration were the weakest'.[4] Without questioning his judgement, which was not often wrong, some of the points that were made are worth looking at.

There were three main classes of objection, and the first

related to experience in other countries. Faced with the imminent prospect of a registration system being established, men began, apparently for the first time, to take an interest in comparative institutions. Those who opposed the system root and branch looked to Ireland, while those who thought it was a good thing to do but could have been done more cheaply looked to France. In Ireland a system of registration had been established as far back as 1727,[5] and a century of experience furnished plenty of ammunition for those who believed that the Whigs' innovation would not achieve any of the things hoped for from it. Elections in Ireland were not noticeably more orderly or better conducted than those in England, impersonation was rife, and the Irish electorate was even more obviously subject to manipulation by attorneys than the English one. To these charges no absolutely convincing answer could be made. Ministers were unable to lay their fingers on any fundamental difference between the two systems, and, after referring to the refinements of the new scheme, they were forced to rely heavily upon some supposed difference in the standards of behaviour in the two countries.[6] Here, at least, they had popular prejudice on their side, together with the one tiny scrap of evidence which could be found, which was that in the two English constituencies where a proper register was kept and used, Oxford and Cambridge Universities, voting was orderly, impersonation even of the non-residents was unknown, and no attorneys were employed.[7]

Opponents like J. D. Chambers, who took a milder line, argued that the government ought rather to have imitated the system in France. There, the franchise being conditional upon payment of a certain annual sum in taxes, the tax returns automatically constituted an electoral register without additional expense. This was, of course, a criticism of the Whigs' choice of franchise as much as of their choice of a system of registration, and wisely they did not allow themselves to be led away by the search for a cheap and foolproof system of registration into imitating the French model, 'uniform, simple and lucid'[8] as that may have been. The reason is not far to seek. If the franchise were linked to the payment of a certain sum in taxes, then every alteration in the burdens of the state and the levels of taxation would affect the electorate. Every budget would become either an enfranchising Bill, if it increased taxes, or a disfranchising Bill if it reduced them. Although this had not, apparently, ever happened in France, the Whigs seem to have feared that a Tory government would reduce taxes in the year before a general election and increase them again after-wards. As for the Whigs themselves, since they were committed both to an extension of the franchise and to a reduction of taxes, the proposal would have wrong-footed them completely, and was one that could not be entertained for a moment.

The second class of objections centred upon the Whigs' choice of the overseers of the poor and the barristers as their instruments. Some Members feared political bias on the part of the overseers, many voiced doubts as to their ability to prepare the draft lists, and towards the end of a long and hot day during the committee stage of the Bill in August, Baring remarked acidly that 'the Overseers of the poor were to fulfil all the provisions of a clause which had puzzled the greatest lawyers in the House to understand it'.[9] To this Althorp replied that the overseers already prepared the jury lists and the population returns, and that there was no reason to suppose that the Bill would require a degree of impartiality or of competence which overseers generally were incapable of supplying.[10] The more serious argument relating to the overseers concerned the pro-posal to make their expenses a charge upon the poor rates.[11] In the first place there were a large number of people who paid poor rates who were not likely to qualify for the vote, and it was not clear why they should be called upon to pay for the privileges of those who did. In the second place, and in the long run more important as conditioning attitudes and sharpening class distinctions, whatever the legal position might be, the poor regarded the money collected from the poor rate as belonging to them by right — to be expended upon their necessities. In the back streets, where men were not enfranchised anyway, and under the new legislation would be unable even to make objection to those whose names were on the list, the decision to employ the overseers and to pay their expenses out of the poor rate looked like a raid on the bank. To this the Whigs made no answer at all: it was an early example of that insensitivity to the poor which was soon to be indelibly burned into working-class consciousness by the deportation of the Tolpuddle 'martyrs', and the adoption of the less-eligibility principle in the work-houses of the new poor-law unions established under the Act of

1834. And, just to drive the point home, the registration was to take place every year, and every year the poor were to be reminded that they were excluded from the electoral club and made to feel that the more the registration cost the less there was for them.

The overseers' work was to be checked, complemented and perfected by the new tribe of 160 revising barristers. Politically it was a shrewd move to offer the legal profession an interest in the passage of the Reform Bill. But here, at least, the opposition at once found a large target to shoot at, for the Bill said that the nominations of the revising barristers were to be subject to the approval of the Lord Chancellor. Brougham, whose election for the West Riding in 1830 was widely thought to have precipitated the collapse of Wellington's administration, was, perhaps, *le plus terrible des enfants terribles* of Grey's administration. Even after they had persuaded him to go to the House of Lords, Ministers themselves remained anxious about his ambitions, and the Cabinet needed little prodding to redraft the Bill in such a way as to leave the nominations of the revising barristers with the senior judge upon each circuit.

The third class of objections, and the ones most commonly expressed, were that the new registration system would throw 'the public mind of England into an annual ferment',[12] and lead to an enormous increase in the activity of party political associations. Far from ensuring that passion was confined to the two days allowed for the poll at a contested election, and that the examination of claims and objections took place in a calm and judicial atmosphere, 'a little . . . election' would be got up every year at the time of registration.[13] In short, as Brougham himself trenchantly put it, after he had left the Reformers and changed sides, by offering all the excitement of an election without having a calming effect upon the people, the new registration system 'contained in itself all the evils of annual Parliaments, without any of their advantages'.[14] The whole scheme would play into the hands of the political unions, which would press their demand for annual Parliaments by turning every registration *de facto* into an annual polling of the people.[15]

The Reformers regarded this as a risk which had to be run, and it was not until 1845 that experience enabled *The League* newspaper to put a different point of view. Arguing that the

registration clauses of the Reform Act had indeed effected a
revolution in British politics, *The League* demonstrated how the
new machinery had 'transferred the franchise to the family of
the sober, patient, plodding virtues'.[16] 'There never was a
constitution, resting ultimately on a popular basis, which
exacted from the people so large an amount of what may be
called the unpopular virtues — forethought, patience, calcu-
lation ....'[17] The country could never again 'be taken by
storm (as in 1830) in the power of a good popular "cry"'.[18]
The cry was good for nothing without the votes, the votes were
good for nothing if they were not registered, and they never
would be registered unless people attended to it. However much
excitement there might be at the annual registrations, the
registration procedures would be spread out over a period of
months and would lack the obvious focal point of an election.
The fact was, then, according to *The League*, that the Reform
Act had put 'hustings eloquence and popular excitement in
Schedule A'.[19] There was an element of special pleading about
all this, of course, for by 1845 the Anti-Corn Law League had
turned the registration into a round-the-calendar activity, as we
shall see in Chapter 5. Nor was there any obvious reason why
the same kind of popular pressures which had made an impact
upon the voters under the old system in 1830, and still more in
1831, could not reach the electors after 1832. But with his
marvellous flair for expression the editor of *The League* had
almost certainly put into words much of what was in the minds
of the Reformers when they attempted to divorce scrutiny from
passion in 1832.

Opponents who were worried by the prospect of an annual
tumult were already taking it for granted that quiet, respectable
people would not want to make objections, and that party
political agents would take an increasing interest in the annual
registration, just as they had done in Ireland. Colonel Wood
forecast that in future every county Member would have to
employ an agent in every hundred, and J. D. Chambers anticipated that, in future, a 'retained agent, or solicitor' would be
found in every district.[20] Baring neatly put together the two
fears of annual ferment and undue interference by party agents
when he said that 'the end of the matter would be, that the list
would be prepared by some lawyer for his own purposes. He
would be met by the lawyers of the opposite party, and the

collision that would take place would prolong the contests from one year to another without intermission'.[21]

The answer to this had already been given by the Select Committee of 1826–7, which had welcomed the prospect that, wherever a contest was anticipated, party initiative would act to purify the registers.[22] But the Select Committee of 1826–7 was ahead of its time: nobody liked parties, and few people were yet prepared to admit that there was a legitimate place for them in the electoral system. Just how far their importance would increase, and just how unacceptable any increase in their importance would be, remained to be seen. In the meantime, people, politicians and party agents alike were busy digesting the precise details of the registration clauses of the Reform Act. Since these were to condition the future course of British politics, some account must now be given of them here, and right from the start the point to grasp is that, because the franchises were different, the procedures were not exactly the same in the boroughs and in the counties.

It is generally said, in historians' short-hand, that in the boroughs the Reform Act instituted a £10 householder franchise. The phrase requires elaboration. In the first place, the franchise was not restricted to residential property. The Act actually specified 'House, Warehouse, Counting-house, Shop or other building',[23] and the value of shop and office property, like the value of house property, varied from one end of the country to the other. In the second place, the Act imposed four more conditions which the £10 householder must satisfy before his name could be placed upon the register of electors. The first was that he must have been in possession of or 'occupied' property of sufficient value as owner or tenant for at least twelve months previous to the 31 July in each year; the second was that he must have resided within seven miles of the borough for at least six months previous to 31 July; and the third and the fourth were that he must before 20 July have paid all poor rates and assessed taxes due from him up to the preceding 6 April.[24] The inhabitant of a borough, therefore, had to jump not just one hurdle, as the term '£10 householder' suggests, but one leading hurdle followed by four additional ones in succession if he were to qualify to have his name placed upon the register of electors.

Nor were these additional hurdles without effect in

reducing the size of the electorate. The twelve-months possession or occupation qualification, for example, virtually
eliminated Wesleyan Methodist ministers, who were accustomed
to taking up their new stations towards the end of August.
Twenty-three months elapsed before their names could be
placed upon the registers, and, since, by the rules of the
connexion, the maximum time they were permitted to stay in
any one place was three years, they could never hope to see
their names on the register for more than one year in three. The
residence qualification meant that in an age of increasing social
mobility any householder who moved from one borough to
another forfeited his vote in the borough he had left behind him
long before he could acquire another vote in the borough to
which he had gone. That was an inconvenience for which time
would provide a remedy in each individual case: much more
serious in its effects upon the electorate was the requirement
relating to the payment of rates. Many tenants did not pay their
rates directly, but 'compounded' for them through their landlords. The tenants' names remained unknown, therefore, to the
overseers of the poor, and the clause in the Reform Act which
authorised tenants to demand to pay their rates in their own
names remained a dead letter.[25] The tenants who would have
liked to pay their own rates and secure the vote lacked the
courage simultaneously to ask their landlords for equivalent
reductions in their rents, and the result was that tens of
thousands of £10 householders thus remained unregistered.
Finally, both the requirement to have paid the rates and the
requirement to have paid the assessed taxes (most £10 houses
had more than seven windows and were liable to the window
tax)[26] meant that in any recession large numbers of householders who were in arrears were wiped off the electoral
registers, and in 1846, which was not a bad year, 18,873 of the
498,425 £10 householders known to the overseers in England
and Wales were omitted from the lists for non-payment of
assessed taxes.[27]

The qualifications had been inserted with the instrument in
mind, and in most towns the overseers of the poor were well
able to attend to them. They knew, from their rate books, the
value of each property, they had a pretty shrewd idea whether
the occupant had satisfied the requirements as to length of
possession and residence, they knew, obviously, whether he had

paid his poor rates, and they were given power to inspect the lists kept by the commissioners of assessed taxes.[28] By 31 July, then, in each year, the overseers of each parish were to be ready with a draft list of the names of persons qualified, printed in alphabetical order.[29] Year by year they were required to omit names and to add them, on their own authority, and no man whom they deemed eligible could avoid having his name placed upon the list. Simultaneously the town clerk was responsible for drawing up a list of freemen,[30] and in the boroughs this first part of the registration procedure took the form of what contemporaries called an automatic or self-acting system.

The overseers' and the town clerk's lists were to be exhibited at the door of every church and chapel,[31] and an interval was allowed until 25 August during which those who had been included but were wrongly described might 're-claim', while those who had been omitted might claim, and anyone whose name was on the list or who had made a claim might object to any name which he thought ought not to be there.[32] In the boroughs an objector was not required to serve notice of his objection upon the person he was objecting to, and it seems to have been taken for granted that in a compact community a voter had only himself to blame if he failed to keep his eyes open and to read notices. After 25 August further lists of claims and objections were to be published. The original lists, together with the lists of claims and objections were then to be handed to the revising barrister, whose court was to be held, after due notice of at least three days had been given, at any time between 15 September and 25 October. The overseers and the town clerk were required to attend the revising barrister's court, when claims and objections would be heard. Any man against whom there was an objection and who failed to appear to defend his vote was to be struck off automatically, and even those who did appear to defend their votes were likely to be at a disadvantage, because they had no means of knowing in advance the nature of the objection. When the objection was to a wrong description, however, either of the elector, or of his address, or of the property in respect of which he was qualified, the revising barrister was to have power to correct mistakes.[33] When all the cases had been heard, and all the entries in the list had been corrected, the entire list of names was to be put together, parish by parish, and serially numbered. The register was then to be handed to the returning officer to be printed, and to come into force on 1 November.[34]

In the counties there were no fewer than four main categories of voters: the freeholders at forty shillings and above, the copyholders at £10, the leaseholders at £10 for any unexpired part of a lease originally granted for a term of sixty years and at £50 for any unexpired part of a lease originally granted for twenty years, and, finally, the occupiers or tenants at will paying £50 per annum, who were inserted upon amendment by the notorious Chandos Clause.[35] These four groups spawned such a bewildering variety of descriptions in the registers that in due course George Wilson, the Chairman of the Anti-Corn Law League, was able to hand the Select Committee of 1846 a list of what he called

576 different freehold qualifications
400 different copyhold qualifications
250 different leasehold qualifications
 50 different occupation qualifications

making a grand total of 1276 in all.[36] These basic franchises were not, however, diluted by the registration clauses to the extent that they were in the boroughs. There was a possession qualification of six months in the case of the freeholder and the copyholder, and in the case of the lease-holder and the occupier an occupation qualification of twelve months,[37] which, in practice, since leases normally ran from Michaelmas Day (29 September), became one of twenty-two months. But anyone coming into possession of his property through inheritance, marriage, promotion to an office or presentation to a benefice was entitled to come onto the register immediately[38] — an interesting example of a system which was geared to property also favouring certain specific and rather old-fashioned modes of acquiring it. Freeholders for life under £10 were expected to reside,[39] but there was no general residence requirement, which, given their habit of spending half the year in London, would have disfranchised the upper classes completely, and throughout the county franchises there was no requirement to have paid rates and taxes.[40]

In the boroughs the overseers were dealing with something visible, and, indeed, unconcealable. They could tell at a glance which was a £10 house, and if they were in doubt they could employ a surveyor. In the counties it was impossible for the overseers to inspect every lease, and there would have been resistance to any clause empowering them to do so, so great was the secrecy with which property in land was surrounded. Consequently the overseers (although they were not actually forbidden to add names) could not be expected to add and omit names on their own authority every year as they did in the boroughs. Instead they were required to give notice on 20 June in each year inviting persons believing themselves to be entitled to vote to send in their claims by 20 July. These claims were to be added to the previous year's list, to make a new draft list, upon which the overseers were to put a mark against any name to which they themselves took exception. This draft was to be published on 31 July, and after that the procedure in the counties was to follow exactly the same timetable as that in the boroughs. Up to 25 August the list was to remain open for objections by the public, and in the counties, as distinct from the boroughs, an objector was required to give notice of objection – though not the ground of his objection – to the person to whom he objected. Between 15 September and 25 October the lists were to be revised by the barristers, and on 1 November the new lists were to come into force.[41]

The main difference between the procedure in the counties and that in the boroughs was that in the counties the system was not self-acting, and there was little likelihood of an elector's name being placed on the list without his making a claim. Similarly, once it had been placed upon the list there was no way in which it could be erased until an objection was made. In the counties, then, a double inertia operated, and, in the absence of any stimulus, there were likely to be many people omitted from the county lists who ought to have been on them, and many others included in them who ought not to have remained there. To this extent, then, much the same criticism might be made of the Act of 1832 as was made of the Act of 1788 – that it was not equal to its purpose. In the counties even more, perhaps, than in the boroughs, the formulation and prosecution of claims and objections, which took place in August, September and October every year, when MPs, who were exhausted at the end of the session, were accustomed to go away on holiday to shoot grouse (August), partridge

(September) and pheasant (October), were bound to fall into the hands of party agents. A stigma attached to this work, and the timing of the registration procedures might almost have been chosen to enable Members to wash their hands of what was being done in their names. The success or failure of the machinery invented in 1832 would depend very largely upon the hundreds of solicitors retained by the parties in the constituencies, who, as party agents, since the constitution knew no parties, were not even mentioned in the Act.

3 A Sort of Battlefield

All over the country contemporaries were glad to find that, after the initial registration in 1832, 'the work of the two following years was performed with tolerable facility and expedition. ... It was pretty generally pronounced that the registration clauses of the reform act worked well upon the whole, and that both the expense and the inconvenience of the revision would proceed for some years in a diminishing ratio.'[1] The number of days occupied by the revising barristers in England and Wales fell from 3662 in 1832 to 2632 in 1833 and 2585 in 1834, and the cost to the Treasury decreased from £30,400 in 1832 to £22,520 in 1834.[2]

Party testimony is suspect, but there seems to be pretty general agreement that in this short period of calm 'the Reformers, lulled into a destructive and deceitful sense of security, most grievously neglected the registration',[3] while the Tories set up 'Registration Associations' in many constituencies, and made a more 'diligent use of the opportunities afforded by the Reform Act to obtain the franchise'.[4] We do not know whether some Tory optimist had a word in the ear of the King and informed him when the new electoral registers came into force. But what better explanation is there for the fact that, in November 1834, when the Reformers still had a majority of over 200 in the House of Commons, William IV seized the pretext afforded by Althorp's elevation to the House of Lords, and dismissed Grey's successor, Melbourne, and his Ministry? Peel, who had been watching the progress of the registration and biding his time, thought the King had acted prematurely, but did not condemn the royal *coup d'état*. Without hesitation he undertook to come to the King's aid and to form a government. Then, being unable, obviously, to survive in the existing House of Commons, he dissolved Parliament and called a general election for January 1835.

By identifying himself with the King's action Peel made it appear premeditated, and raised the party political temperature to a peak. Neither side in the House of Commons had appeared united in 1833—4. But all parties now believed that it was no mere struggle for party politics they had to engage in, 'but a great and resolute struggle to preserve the existence of the constitution'.[5] On one side, the romantic Ultras, who had still not forgiven Peel for his part in the emancipation of the Roman Catholics in 1829, could no longer resist this appeal by a monarch-in-distress for rescue from the 'Destructives'. They rejoined the main body of a reinvigorated Conservative party, which emerged from the general election with approximately 290 seats out of 658 — and many others doubtful.[6] On the other, the Whigs, appalled by the parallel with George III's action in dismissing Fox in 1783 and by the prospect of another forty years of Tory misrule,[7] made common cause, first with the Radicals, who began to revive the political unions, and then with the Irish, without whose aid they could not revenge themselves upon the King. This, in turn, brought the Tories out in a fit of Britishness and anti-Popery, and, for months after the Whigs recovered office in April, the excitement of party politics remained at fever pitch.

Throughout 1835 men's minds kept turning to the registration. The January election placed Peel with power so nearly within his grasp that it was widely supposed that, if defeated in the House of Commons, he would try the effect of a second dissolution. Peel himself, however, seems to have doubted whether a second dissolution upon the same register would produce an improved result. When the Whigs returned to power it was equally widely supposed that they, too, might dissolve upon an appeal to the people.[8] These speculations came to an abrupt end, however, with the results of two by-elections in May, when Lord John Russell, Home Secretary and Leader of the House of Commons, was defeated (upon seeking re-election after accepting an office of profit under the Crown) in South Devonshire, and the Staffordshire seat vacated by E. J. Littleton (when he accepted a peerage as Lord Hatherton) was also lost by the Whigs to the Tories. For the remainder of the session the Whigs sought to consolidate their position and 'to save the Reform Act'. In the constituencies they followed their opponents' lead and organised Registration Associations, Reform Associations and Reform Registration Associations of their own. In London they established a central Reform Association situated in Cleveland Row, and founded a Reform Club where they and their Radical and Irish allies dined together for the first time. In Parliament they proceeded resolutely with a Bill to reform the old municipal corporations, which still possessed undue influence over the return of Members of Parliament to represent the boroughs of England and Wales. These measures filled the Reformers with a revived sense of confidence in themselves, and when the Municipal Corporations Bill reached the statute book, and everyone knew that henceforward the new town councils would be elected upon a simple ratepaying franchise, Joseph Parkes, the Whig agent, declared that no Tory majority could ever again be obtained in the House of Commons.[9] But the Tories in their turn had good reason to suppose that the Whigs' alliance with O'Connell would not be popular in England, Wales and Scotland, and in the somewhat unusual circumstance that both parties were confident, simultaneously, that the current was running their way, no effort was spared, on either side, to secure a majority upon the new electoral registers to be compiled in 1835. Both parties were determined to make all the objections they could, and to make all the claims they could, and the dramatic increase in party activity which then took place tested the new registration machinery almost to the point of collapse.

There were four columns in the registers, and a mistake in any one of them might provide grounds for disqualification, so that the scope for making objections was wide. Furthermore the framers of the Act had recognised that the procedure for making objections would be open to abuse, and that, in particular, there would be the risk of 'speculative', 'vexatious', and 'wholesale' objections. But they had unwisely trusted to the good sense of their countrymen to avoid these things, and none of the obvious safeguards had been written into the Act. Subsequent attempts to remedy the deficiencies of the Act had not been pressed,[10] and in the autumn of 1835 the position remained that in both boroughs and counties a voter who failed to appear before the revising barrister to defend his vote lost it automatically. There was every incentive, then, for the parties to make speculative objections which could not be substantiated but which could not fail of their object either, if the person objected to failed to appear in court. There was no provision for costs to be awarded against the vexatious objector, and two kinds of vexatious objection became common, first against those living at a distance and second against those who were prominent. In 1835 the Reformers objected to Sir Robert Peel's vote in North Warwickshire,[11] while the Tories in Bloomsbury went one better (or rather worse) and objected to the votes of Lord John, Lord Wriothesley, Lord Edward, Lord Charles James Fox and Lord William Russell, or 'the Duke of Bedford's faggots', as they were called.[12] Further, there was no limit to the number of persons against whom an elector might object. In 1835, 'a gentleman of London', making fun of what seemed to most of his contemporaries to be a lamentable state of affairs, 'announced in the papers his intention of opening a "new trade" . . . establishing a firm for making objections to *every* voter upon the lists in the county for which his own name is inserted, and then accepting a small sum of money from each person to forego the objection!'[13] There was, indeed, at this time, as George Wilson, the Chairman of the Anti-Corn Law League later told the Select Committee of 1846, nothing to stop a man from purchasing a forty-shilling freehold in every county and objecting to every other (county) voter in the land.[14].

In 1835 reports came in from all over the country that the Tories had objected to every single Liberal voter in a whole street, and that the Destructives had objected to every farmer in North Warwickshire.[15] It is impossible to say exactly how many objections were made, because the newspapers did not print reports according to a consistent pattern, and all we can learn from the official reports is that the proceedings in the revision courts lasted 3838 days and cost £32,086.[16] But even in a tiny county like the Isle of Wight the parties alone sustained 264 objections. In North Wiltshire they lodged 667 and in East Surrey 671. In Norfolk they excelled themselves with 1363 objections in the Eastern division and 1752 in the West. In South Devonshire, which was still in a ferment after the by-election in May, the parties and the overseers between them lodged 2324 objections. In Middlesex they made 3154, and in the West Riding the figure topped 7000.[17] In the boroughs, too, the figures appear to have increased three- and fourfold over the previous year.

Faced with objections upon a scale for which there was no precedent, it soon became clear that 160 barristers, inadequately briefed by the Home Secretary, proceeding simultaneously and acting independently, could not be expected straightaway to step into identical interpretations of the law. Many barristers inevitably took short cuts through their work and came up with a crop of contradictory decisions, being unable to agree, for example, whether it was necessary, in the counties, for an objector to serve notice of objection by himself or whether he might employ a servant to deliver it for him, and whether it was permissible for the forms of objection to be signed first, when blank, and then filled in afterwards.[18] More fundamentally still, in the blaze of publicity to which the revising barristers were now exposed, it turned out that even the basic requirements for the franchise, which had seemed clear enough when they were before Parliament, were susceptible of widely different interpretations in the revision courts when they were explored and scrutinised with partisan ingenuity.

In determining whether a man claiming a borough vote did or did not live in a £10 house, one barrister would accept the word of a landlord, a second would require the tenant to produce a receipt for the rent, and a third would pin his judgement upon the evidence of a surveyor. The £10 householder was required to have been in occupation of his house for twelve months before the 31 July: in one constituency the barrister ruled that the voter must occupy the entire house, to the exclusion of tenants and lodgers; in another it was held that he might occupy a part and let a part. The six-months residence requirement led to complicated questions about business trips and holidays, and raised the question whether it was necessary for the elector to have resided in the borough in person, or whether it was sufficient for him to have maintained his family, or even his servant, there. Even the apparently easily determined requirement to have paid the rates turned out to be more difficult than anyone had foreseen. Some barristers held that payment by anybody in the occupier's name was sufficient, others that the payment, if not by the occupier, must be by somebody expecting to be repaid (i.e. not by a party agent), and others again that 'a good payment can only be by the occupier himself'. 'Further, as the whole of these rates are directed to be paid, it has been made a question, decided differently by different barristers, whether the voter is not necessitated to discharge all arrears on the premises incurred by any person who preceded him.' Similarly, in the revision courts for the counties, one barrister would demand to inspect a freeholder's title deeds, a second would be satisfied with the draft of a conveyance, and a third would accept the man's oath, unless impugned.[19]

Objecting to the votes of opponents was one thing: mobilising all the votes you could on your own side was the other. Here lay the real battleground between the parties in the English counties, where the Tories had recovered twenty-nine seats in January.[20] Some idea of what was involved can be obtained when we consider that, while the borough electorate in England increased gradually from 275,151 in 1832 to 319,396 in 1839,[21] the county electorate (excluding the Isle of Wight), which had risen slowly from 342,970 in 1832 to 357,053 in 1834, now jumped in a single year by over 80,000 to 437,931 in 1835. That is to say that over half the increase of approximately 157,000 which took place between 1832 and 1864 occurred in a single year.[22]

Faced with this astonishing increase, historians have been inclined to suppose that the numbers were composed, as Parkes and other Whig agents alleged,[23] almost entirely of £50 tenants at will or 'occupiers' of farms whose qualifications were being manufactured by the Tories under the Chandos Clause. This view will not stand serious examination. Even in 1839, the first year for which statistics covering the whole country and breaking the electorate down into its component elements were obtained, the 99,886 occupiers comprised less than two-ninths of the total of 456,030 county electors in England, and were outnumbered almost three to one by the freeholders.[24] An examination of individual county registers suggests that, after the first registration, in many counties the £50 tenants at will came onto the registers rather more slowly than other classes of voters. Nowhere is this more evident than in Warwickshire, Parkes's own county, where he continued to take a personal interest in superintending the registration for the two divisions. In the Northern half of the county the electorate increased by

74·40 per cent, from 3730 in 1832 to 6505 in 1835, and the occupiers increased during the same period by 25·46 per cent, from 793 to 995, declining in three years from 21·26 to 15·29 per cent of the electorate. In the Southern half of the county, where the electorate increased by 56·74 per cent, from 2550 in 1832 to 3997 in 1835, the occupiers increased by 40·37 per cent, from 867 to 1217. There are other parts of the country where the pattern appears to have been the same. In West Suffolk the electorate increased by 48·89 per cent, from 3326 in 1832 to 4952 in 1835, while the occupiers increased by 41·52 per cent during the same period, from 843 to 1193; and in West Surrey, where the electorate increased more slowly, by 26·65 per cent, from 2912 in 1832 to 3688 in 1836, the occupiers increased by 22·85 per cent, from 477 to 586. In Buckinghamshire, on the other hand, where the 12·36 per cent increase in the number of occupiers between 1832 and 1836 outran the 7·22 per cent increase in the electorate, the increase in the overall numbers was unusually small, from 5306 to 5760; and in East Surrey, where the electorate increased by 68·51 per cent between 1832 and 1835, from 3150 to 5308, and the occupiers increased by 105·32 per cent, from 432 in 1832 to 887 in 1835, the greater part of the increase consisted of business and residential property to the south of London, and of mansions beside the river tenanted by persons of substantial means who chose to rent property by the year and whose votes could in no sense be described as dependent. Thus in Clapham the fifty-pounders increased from forty-three in 1832 to 141 in 1835, and in Richmond they increased from nineteen to forty-six. It is impossible to distinguish residential from farm property with certainty in every case, but an attempt to do so suggests that over the whole constituency the occupying farmers increased much more slowly during the same period, from 125 to 169.

Myths of the Left die hard; and the truth is that, until recently, historians have accepted all too readily the view — first expressed in the debates in Parliament in August 1831 — of the tenant at will as a farm animal bred by the great landowners for herding through the annual political sheep fair.[25] Unquestionably there were places, as party agents like Parkes alleged, where landlords surveyed their estates in order to ascertain how many votes they could create, and in many cases care was taken to ensure that a farm yielding £100 per annum was divided in order to secure two votes. But searches among the actual registers of county voters indicate that the true picture was more complicated than this.

In the first place, many tenants at will were not farmers. This was particularly noticeable in an area like East Surrey, but, even in a more purely agricultural area, like Suffolk or Sussex, a substantial number of occupiers were qualified in respect of what might be regarded as 'industrial' properties — mills, forges and the like. In the second place, even when a tenant at will was a farmer that did not mean that his tenancy had necessarily been drafted disreputably in order to manufacture a faggot vote. Even upon the large estate the tenant at will had a role to play in contemporary agricultural practice, and the large landowners were not, in any case, the only ones whose actions created tenants at will. In parts of South Warwickshire, where there were many small properties, almost every village yields an example of a small freeholder having apparently created a tenancy in favour of his son. Thus, in Burnington, Thomas Sheldon senior qualified in respect of the freehold and Thomas Sheldon junior in respect of the occupation of the same farm, while, in Cherrington, Edward Timms senior and Edward Timms junior, and, in Priors Marston, Robert Pratt senior and Robert Pratt junior stood in the same relationship. Whether, in Tysoe, Thomas Middleton junior really did own the freehold, and Thomas Middleton senior occupy the land as tenant, as the register says, or whether this was a slip which a negligent party agent failed to notice, it is impossible to say.

These examples are all taken from the original register of 1832, and in South Warwickshire the creation of tenancies at will was presumably part of the normal pattern of family life and inheritance in the countryside. But, even in areas where customs were different, any small farmer with a freehold who left the country for the town might be inclined to keep his options open by putting in a tenant at will upon the property he had left behind him; and any businessman or professional man who made a fortune in the town might purchase a farm in the country and install a tenant at will. In both cases owner and occupier both qualified for a vote. Thus at Stockton, in South Warwickshire, Thomas Lamb of Regent Street, London, quali-fied in respect of freehold land in the occupation of William

Griffin, and William Griffin also qualified in respect of 'rental occupier of land'. Similarly, at Aldingbourne in West Sussex, William Watkins of 11 Sackville Street, London, qualified in respect of copyhold house and land, 'Thomas Woolley tenant', while Thomas Woolley also qualified as a tenant at will at £50. At Arundel, Price Bowen of 'Lanrwst', Denbigh, qualified in respect of freehold windmill and premises, 'Charles Bartlett and William Watkins tenants', and Charles Bartlett and William Watkins both qualified as tenants.[26] In short, there were often perfectly normal and respectable reasons for creating tenants at will, and, while some large landowners may have been able to create substantial numbers of dependent votes, many of the dependent votes which were created were singletons.

Once the tenants at will had been enfranchised in 1832 there was nothing improper in seeking to bring as many as possible of them onto the registers. And what seems to have happened in 1835 is not that an army of dependent farmers was marched onto the registers in order to deprive the English people of their liberties, but that owners of property of all descriptions who had not previously been registered were moved by the excitement of the times, or prevailed upon by the parties, to make a claim to vote. The result was, for the first time, to bring the registers up to what might be regarded as a 'true' level, and by far the greater number of those who were registered for the first time in 1835 were, in fact, freeholders. Included in those freeholders there was at least one substantial category of persons among whom it is not unreasonable to presume that the Reformers enjoyed a numerical advantage. The 'urban free-holders' were mainly of two kinds: a relatively small number of adult males who possessed undeveloped plots within the boundaries of boroughs which did not qualify them for borough votes as £10 householders, but which did qualify them as forty-shilling freeholders in the counties; and a relatively large and increasing number of men who occupied one house in which they dwelt and qualified as £10 householders in the boroughs, and who owned an office, shop or workshop from which they conducted their businesses and by virtue of which they qualified as forty-shilling freeholders in the counties. Further and more detailed research will be necessary before we can estimate their numbers at this time, but the custom of 'living over the shop' was already beginning to be broken — round London especially — and, as the practice of living in one place and working in another became more common, more and more independent tradesmen and businessmen were able to qualify in both a borough and a county constituency. In 1850 the urban freeholders were recorded as comprising almost exactly one-fifth of the county electorate in England and Wales. Unlike the £50 tenants at will, they were extremely unevenly distributed, being concentrated round the large towns, and their impact was very different from one county, or one division of a county, to another. Thus, in 1850 there were 2054 urban freeholders among an electorate of 7444 in the Northern division of Cheshire, and only 589 among an electorate of 8070 in the Southern division. In East Surrey there were 1970 among an electorate of 6489, and in West Surrey a mere 150 among one of 3906. In counties like Bedfordshire, where there were 368 among 4071, they were few; and in counties like Middlesex, where in the register for 1851 there were 8481 among 14,610, they were many.[27]

The vast majority of freeholds were landed, house or shop properties, but a freehold was not necessarily one of these, and in 1835 the revising barristers were confronted with a barrage of claims made mainly upon behalf of two other categories of persons: the shareholders in commercial and industrial enterprises, and the possessors of life interests in schools, almshouses, hospitals, churches and the like.

The claims made upon behalf of shareholders represented an astonishing range of business interests. For example, in Kent a claim was made on behalf of 250 men who possessed a right in the oyster fishery.[28] Round London claims were lodged on behalf of the seventy-two shareholders in the New Leather Market at Bermondsey,[29] the ninety shareholders in Exeter Hall,[30] and on behalf of the shareholders in the New River Company. In the north of England the favourite form of property appears to have been a share in a cemetery. Clearly, if these sorts of claims were successful, the theoretical possibilities of manufacturing votes by splitting property into as many shares as possible, each of the minimum size to create a forty-shilling freehold, would be enormous, and the capital value of the New River Company would be sufficient, if parcelled out into as many shares as possible, to manufacture ten or twelve thousand voters in Hertfordshire and as many more in Middlesex.[31]

It had long been accepted that neither corporations nor individual members of bodies corporate could vote, and for that reason neither Oxford colleges nor individual Fellows of Oxford colleges qualified as such to vote at elections for knights of the shire. More recently it had been decided that in cases where men joined their stocks of capital together to form a company, and that company bought property, the property belonged to the corporation, while the individual shareholdings remained part of the personal estates of the participants, and thus conferred no vote, which was why, in due course, the construction of railways made no impact upon the size of the electorate. But there was another type of commercial or industrial enterprise, in which the owners of real estate combined to appoint a corporation to manage their property for them, and there the individual shares constituted freeholds and might indeed create votes.[32]

In theory the broad outline of the law was clear, but in practice the distinctions raised were of almost infinite complexity. Faced with the problems involved in determining what kinds of property they were being asked to pronounce upon, the revising barristers came, once again, to what appeared to the general public, at least, to be contradictory decisions. The oyster fishermen lost their claim, the seventy-two shareholders in the New Leather Market were accepted, one of the ninety shareholders in Exeter Hall was taken on board his country's electoral ship and the other eighty-nine were left behind on the quayside, and shareholders in the New River Company were accepted by the revising barristers for Middlesex and rejected by the revising barristers for Hertfordshire. In the north the same patchy pattern continued. One revising barrister considered 'the proprietors of a cemetery fit holders of the elective franchise', while another could 'perceive no life or sense in such a defunct qualification'.[33] In the West Riding Edward Baines, the Member for Leeds, succeeded in his claim to vote for a share in a cemetery, while in Manchester the shareholders in a cemetery in Rusholme Road were rejected.[34] In West Sussex an examination of the register reveals voters qualified in respect of shares in the Gas Light and Coke Company, and in respect of the Arundel Canal. In East Surrey the Surrey Iron Railway supported several votes, and here, as elsewhere, shareholders in waterworks, gasworks and bridges appear to have enjoyed a relatively easy passage to the electoral registers. Thus the number of electors in East Surrey qualified in respect of shares in Putney Bridge increased from six in 1832 to twenty-two in 1835 — and ultimately to sixty-three in 1838, when William Gilmore Bolton, of 25 Austin Friars, London, first qualified in respect of '1—10th of a half of a 30th Freehold share' — which must surely take precedence as the most famous vote in all Surrey. Even that did not, however, exhaust the political possibilities of the bridge, which spanned the river between Surrey and Middlesex, and in 1837, when the registers for the two counties can be compared, there were thirty-four shareholders in the bridge registered in Putney and qualified to vote in Surrey, thirty-three of whom were also to be found among the forty-one shareholders registered in Fulham and qualified to vote in Middlesex.

Round London, at any rate, a majority of the claims made upon behalf of shareholders owning real estate supporting enterprises of this kind appear to have been presented by the Tories and opposed by Liberal agents. All over the country the tally of life interests, too, almost certainly told heavily in favour of the Tories. Thomas Knox DD, who qualified for Middlesex in respect of his annual stipend, secured against lands in St Pancras, as 'master for life of Tonbridge School', came from a Whig family. But John Image and John Vane, who as Senior Fellow and Second Senior Fellow at Dulwich College qualified in both Surrey and Middlesex in respect of annual stipends derived from freehold lands and houses on both sides of the river, the residents of almshouses like Thompson's Hospital, Petworth, and retired officers living in service quarters at Greenwich and Woolwich (whose claims were in fact rejected because they could be thrown out at a day's notice[35]) all had an interest in the conservative ethic. All these groups put together, however, counted for less than that greatest of all manufacturers of life interests, the Established Church. The 11,000 and more ordained clergymen of the Church of England who had been presented to livings possessed freeholds, and were strategically distributed through all the parishes in the country. They had been singled out for favourable treatment in the Act of 1832, and had found their way onto the registers without delay. Now, in 1835, attempts were made to reinforce them both with the parish clerks, many of whose appointments were for life, and whose salaries, in excess of forty shillings per annum, were secured against land and buildings; and with the sextons, many of whom enjoyed the same privileges.

Against this array of Tory voters the Reformers had hitherto been able to muster only a small number of Dissenting ministers. A Dissenting minister who could prove that his appointment was for life, and that he received an income arising directly out of the profits on land and buildings or the rents of pews, might come onto the register, and in every county there seem to have been some, at least, of the Independents who were able to satisfy these requirements. But the vast majority of Dissenting ministers did not enjoy a secure tenure, and held their positions at the pleasure of their congregations, which put them at an obvious disadvantage compared to clergymen of the Established Church. One Dissenting minister, Mr Greenway, argued with the revising barrister that there was no difference between the position of a man in his case, who could be removed by the vote of a majority of the congregation, and the position of a clergyman of the Church of England, who could, he supposed, be removed from his office by an ecclesiastical court for a breach of discipline.[36] It was indeed a strange situation in which, the more democratic the organisation of a chapel became, and the more nearly a minister was responsible to the congregation, the harder he would find it to substantiate his claim to a place in the political representation of his country.

The ministers of the Dissenting churches being unable to form a counterpoise to the clergy of the Established Church, the Reformers conceived the idea of attempting to qualify the trustees of Dissenting chapels, meeting houses and schools instead. There had already been instances of trustees being accepted onto the electoral registers, even in counties like Buckinghamshire, where one might have supposed that the prejudice against them would have been considerable.[37] But no systematic attempt was made to enrol them before 1835, when the Reformers evidently hoped that the recruitment of such a numerous body would form 'a grand manoeuvre which was to drive the Conservatives entirely off the field'.[38] Everywhere the Dissenting trustees were encouraged to claim the vote, and their success or failure in the revision courts was awaited with the utmost interest — the earliest decisions, in South Lancashire and North Warwickshire, being noticed by local newspapers all over the country.

The trustees of Dissenting chapels and schools were, of course, neither the only trustees in existence, nor the only trustees to claim, and the decision of cases involving trustees confronted the revising barristers with an impossible task, because clause twenty-three of the Reform Act laid down that no trustee should be allowed to qualify unless he were in actual possession or receipt of the rent and profits of an estate, while clause twenty-six enacted that 'notwithstanding anything herein-before contained' no person should be entitled to qualify unless he were in actual possession or receipt of the rent or profits 'for his own use'. Upon this occasion it was those responsible for the drafting of the Act rather than the revising barristers who were to blame for the contradictory interpretations of the law which followed.

One revising barrister ruled that, since no trustee of a Dissenting chapel could possibly be said to enjoy the income of the trust 'for his own use', even if clause twenty-three conferred the right to qualify, which he doubted, clause twenty-six took it away again. Accordingly he excluded all chapel trustees.[39] Another concluded that the legislature could not have been so absurd as to enact something in one clause and to repeal it three clauses later. He construed the words 'for his own use' to mean 'for the use of the trust', and admitted all the chapel trustees he could.[40] In between these two extremes 'moderate' revising barristers thought it would be wrong, in interpreting the Reform Act of 1832, to 'exclude from representation a vast quantity of property and many very valuable interests', and attempted to reconcile the two clauses and to make sense of the Act. Among this group the practice grew up of making a serious inquiry into the exact terms of the trust. Where the trustees were empowered to select upon whom and how to spend the money, their claims to be placed upon the electoral register were accepted. Where, on the other hand, the congregation was empowered to supervise and to direct the trustees, the trustees were treated as 'mere conduit pipes' and their claims were rejected.[41]

The upshot of all this was, even for the revising barristers, an unusually spectacular series of perplexing decisions, which were given the greatest possible publicity in the newspapers. The *Staffordshire Advertiser* (an unusually independent newspaper) noticed that in Birmingham the trustees of the Wesleyan Chapel in Belmont Street had been accepted, while those of a Baptist chapel in North Leicestershire had been rejected.[42] The *Suffolk Chronicle* recorded the rejection of the claims of the nine trustees of a freehold estate supporting a Quaker school, and contrasted this with the good fortune of the trustees of a similar estate in Croydon, Surrey, whose claims had been allowed.[43] Gradually, as the weeks went by, a picture, if not a pattern, emerged. In the West Riding the claims were swept aside. In Lancashire, where the revising barristers evidently made a serious attempt to place a construction upon the statute, the decisions turned on 'nice and almost imperceptible shades of difference',[44] and some claims, at least, were accepted. All through the counties surrounding the great towns, contradiction was piled upon contradiction. In South Leicestershire some claims were accepted, and in North Warwickshire fifty chapel trustees came onto the registers where a year earlier, before they became a burning issue, there had been only seven. In Staffordshire Mr Secker rejected them and Mr Whatley accepted them, while in Middlesex the two revising barristers, Mr Coventry and Mr Martin, disagreed, and asked to be allowed to refer the question to a third[45] before finally settling for a policy of rigour stopping short of exclusion.

As the revision drew to a close it began to appear that the Reformers had suffered a disappointment if not an outright defeat. The letter of the law appeared to be against them, and even those revising barristers who took a favourable view of clause twenty-six and interpreted 'for his own use' to mean 'for the use of the trust' were inclined to take a stern view of clause twenty-three, which restricted the right to qualify to those in actual possession or receipt, and to accept the claims of the one or two trustees who actually handled the money rather than those of the whole body which determined how it should be spent. On 4 November a contributor to the *Morning Chronicle* lamented that there had been 'a pretty general disposition to exclude the trustees of dissenting meeting houses', and the Tory *Norfolk Chronicle* was correct in concluding that this army of Whig auxiliaries, 'whose claims were the confident boast of the party', were 'never likely to be numerous or very efficient at the poll'.[46]

Whether in the long run the Reformers were wise to play the card of the Dissenting chapel trustees, and whether the trustees were wise to let themselves be so played is doubtful. Circumstances could arise in which either the minister of the chapel or the trustees, but not both, might be able to qualify.[47] In these cases the political agent was bound to encourage the trustees, who would have many votes, rather than the minister, who would have one, and thus to complicate, if not to sour, the delicate relations existing between the parts of the chapel body. Even more significant in the life of the Christian church, the visible exploitation, for political purposes, of a body of men who had hitherto been better known for their political neutrality further embittered the relations between the Established Church and the Dissenters. The trustees became caught up in a larger, general, and extremely unedifying struggle between the two sections at a time when the Church was being beguiled by the Oxford Movement and the Dissenters were busy celebrating the three-hundredth anniversary of the Reformation, which they dated from the publication of Coverdale's translation of the Bible (on Sunday 4 October — right in the middle of the revision). Clergymen, of both kinds, had the misfortune of being both easily recognised and easily characterised as Conservatives and Reformers. No occupational group, therefore, was more open to vexatious objections, and in 1835 there seems to have been parish after parish where there was an old score waiting to be paid off. In Rochester an objection was lodged to Dr Hawkins, the Provost of Oriel, who was expunged.[48] In Lambeth an objection was made to the Archbishop of Canterbury, who saved his vote because, although he was a lord of Parliament, he was not a peer of the realm.[49] In Durham objection was made to all the pensioned clergymen, and in Norfolk every clergyman in possession of land originating with Queen Anne's bounty was obliged to defend his vote.[50] Even today, those objections for which there were justifiable grounds and which were successful do not read well. What petty village quarrel lay behind the objection to the incumbent of Mortehoe, Devon, on the ground that he had changed his residence,[51] and to the Reverend Charles Taylor, in consequence of the fact that his name had been inserted in the draft list of voters after it had been affixed to the church door?[52] In this sort of poisoned atmosphere the Conservatives naturally paid the Reformers back in their own coin. The Reverend John Hole of Woolfardisworthy, Devon, was among those taking the initiative in making objections to Liberal votes,[53] and the *Surrey Standard* struck an unusually offensive note, even for 1835, when it referred to 'the Dissenting chapel faggots, all the scum and rakings of sedition and corruption', and praised the Tory agents for their efforts 'to cleanse the constituency from this heterogenous filth' swelling the lists of the Destructives.[54]

It is difficult not to feel sympathy for the revising barristers, who were toiling through a mountain of claims and objections, and who knew that when they had finished the revision of the lists of Parliamentary electors they would be required to revise the first lists of voters for the new town councils established under the Municipal Corporations Reform Act (they were not required to revise them in subsequent years). Nothing, however, should be allowed to disguise the fact that in these circumstances many of the revising barristers found the new element of religious controversy injected into the revision courts the last straw, and that their impartiality snapped under the strain. The *Morning Chronicle* alleged that Dissenting ministers had been disqualified or not 'according to the Reviser's zeal for the Establishment, his notion of the preacher's character, or his satisfaction at his demeanour whilst under examination'. 'A Reviser in a southern county makes war upon the whole confraternity of parish clerks . . . whilst a Reviser in a northern district takes them under his especial protection . . . ',[55] and in North Leicestershire the revising barrister was said in every instance to have decided against the claims of Dissenting ministers and chapel trustees, and to have '*admitted parish clerks paid out of the parish rates*'[56] — i.e. without a freehold.

The leading articles in the *Morning Chronicle* were written by Joseph Parkes and the charges made in them should be repeated with caution, but there were many occasions upon which, if the reporting was accurate, journalists' accusations of politico-religious bias were well-founded. One Revising Barrister opened the proceedings by taking all the cases involving the clergy of the Church of England first, in order to release them to attend to their duties, while pointedly refusing to extend the same favour to the Dissenters.[57] Another ruled that the clause in the Reform Act requiring the overseers' lists of claims and objections to be exhibited upon the door of every church and chapel referred only to the chapels of the Established Church, and that it was unnecessary for the draft lists to be placed upon the doors of Methodist 'and other Dissenting chapels'.[58] In Staffordshire Mr Secker scarcely listened to the arguments advanced in favour of the claim by a Dissenting minister, the Reverend Mr Greenway, and attempted to cut him off by ruling that as he had no freehold he could not vote. When Mr Greenway's lawyer continued to argue the case, Mr Secker decided that 'as the tenure by which Mr Greenway held his office was uncertain, his name must be expunged', and finally, when Mr Greenway himself attempted to carry on where his lawyer had been obliged to leave off, he was silenced by a thunderous 'Name struck out!'[59]

In South Lancashire, Mr Greenwood appears, at the commencement of his circuit, to have tried to act judicially, going out of his way to point out that it was obviously the intention of clause twenty-three of the Reform Act to enfranchise chapel trustees but that the difficulty lay with clause twenty-six, which contradicted it. But as the circuit continued his patience wore thin, and after taking a chapel trust deed back with him to his hotel one night, he discovered that, whatever clauses twenty-three and twenty-six might say, in this particular case the chapel itself had not been in existence long enough to confer the vote. Thereafter he could neither conceal his prejudices nor restrain his passions. 'A grosser fraud was never attemped. . . . It reflects most disgracefully upon a class of religionists who till this time I had thought respectable.' At the next town he came to, the politico-religious affiliation in him got the better of his legal training, and he opened the proceedings by announcing that he would never again decide upon a chapel case until he had examined the deeds (which was reasonable, and even dutiful), because he had been so cheated 'by all parties in chapel trusts, not of one denomination alone, but by methodists, independents, baptists, and people of every denomination' (which was a scandalous thing to say).[60]

When the registration machinery had become law, many people had anticipated that the overseers would prove the weak link, and the revising barristers themselves had not been slow to criticise their humble inferiors, one-third of whom, one barrister alleged, could not read and write.[61] Nobody, however, expected the overseers to be any better than they were, and everything they did, or failed to do, was subject to the scrutiny of the party agents and the revising barristers themselves. Public expectation of the law, however, was rather different. It had been taken for granted in advance that the revising barristers would conduct themselves judicially, without caprice, and without visible bias, and that their decisions would be consistent. When it transpired that one learned gentleman sprang to his conclusion without hearing half the evidence, while another took hours or even days 'to resolve a point that could not puzzle an attorney's clerk five minutes';[62] when it appeared that 'Mr. COVENTRY contradicts Mr. MARTIN; Mr. CRAIG differs from both. What is law in Finsbury is not law in Middlesex; East Surrey and West Kent are enfranchised upon different principles',[63] and that even the revising barristers themselves had so little confidence in their own decisions that they did not expect them to endure from year to year;[64] and above all when it turned out that one revising barrister could not conceal indifference and indecision, while another displayed precipitancy, intemperance, and finally, in the case of the chapel trustees, blatant bias — the general public was shocked.

The revision of 1835 tore the veil off the legal profession, and public concern about the behaviour of the barristers and the fate of the trustees was neatly combined in a parody which appeared in the *Manchester Courier* for 10 October 1835, purporting to report the scenes in the registration courts in 1840.

Barrister (loquitur) — Where is the fellow who calls himself chief magistrate . . . ?

Agent — I cannot say, Sir, but I understand he has gone to Brighton for the benefit of his health.

Barrister — *Brighton! What business has he at Brighton?* Why did he not attend here to procure me proper accommodation?

Agent — He did not think —

Barrister — *Think, Sir, what right has he to think?* I shall write *by this night's post* to the Secretary of State on the subject. Where is the Overseer? Call the Overseer — Oh dear! Oh dear! Do bring the Overseer here. (ore rotundo) The Overseer!

(Enter Overseer. Clock strikes ten)

Barrister — Well, Sir, here you are at last. Do you know how many hours of my valuable time you have consumed by your delay, Sir?

Overseer — I thought —
Barrister — There, you are thinking again. What right have you to think, Sir? Answer my questions. How many objections are there?
Overseer — I think, about —
Barrister — Oh dear! Oh dear! Give me a plain answer. Are there ten or ten thousand?
Overseer — Between the two numbers you have named, Sir.
Barrister — Answer my question plainly, or I will adjourn the Court. . . . Call the first case. (John Adams appears) Who are you Sir?
John Adams — John Adams, Sir, and I come —
Barrister — Answer my questions, Sir, or I will strike your name off the register of voters, and adjourn the court. What is your qualification?
John Adams — A freehold house and land of which I am trustee.
Barrister — You have not sent in your claim as trustee, so better luck next time. I shall strike you off now. Claim next year as trustee. (Exit John Adams).

(Scene changes to another Barrister's room — enter John Smith)

2nd Barrister — What is your qualification?
John Smith — I am trustee with John Adams of a freehold house and land.
2nd Barrister — What is the value?
John Smith — Above £50 a year, which we may apply in any manner we think fit, for the benefit of the . . . trust.
2nd Barrister — Well, Sir! You have claimed as possessor, it would appear, of a freehold house and land, whereas you only have them in trust; but I can alter that.
Agent — Mr. ——— has just struck off John Adams, the co-

trustee, on the ground that this mistake cannot be altered.

2nd Barrister — Can't help that, Sir. Mr. John Smith, yours is a good vote.

(Scene changes — First Barrister's Court, re-enter John Adams)

John Adams — Mr. ———— has just decided, Sir, that my co-trustee has a good vote; but his misdescription is the same as mine.

1st Barrister — How dare you, Sir, come and interrupt me, Sir? What do I care, Sir, for what Mr. ——— decides, or the House of Commons either, Sir? Yours is a bad vote, so you may go and make the best of it (Exit John Adams).

(Scene changes to third Barrister's Court — Enter Joe Fibster)

3rd Barrister — You claim as trustee — how many trustees are there besides yourself?

Joe Fibster — John Adams, John Smith, and Job Wigg.

3rd Barrister — Have you power to repair the property, and is it of sufficient value?

Joe Fibster — Yes.

3rd Barrister — It is clear that this person is . . . a trustee 'to his own use', according to the conveyancing sense of the term, and thus comes within the very letter of the Reform Act. Your vote is allowed Mr. Fibster.

(Scene changes to fourth Barrister's Court — Enter Job Wigg)

4th Barrister — Pray do you pay over the money after deduction of expenses for repairs?

Job Wigg — I do.

4th Barrister — Then you are a conduit pipe, and cannot vote. Were it otherwise the country might be swamped by a quantity of mere water pipes. I erase your name.

The fourth revision drew to a close, and, as the *Manchester Herald* put it, there appeared to be as much difference of opinion as there was three years ago, with the result that 'we have the decision of today reversed by the decision of to-

morrow'.[65] Even an experienced demagogue like Thomas
Wakley was unable to master the law and made a blunder when
he wrote to the editor of the *Morning Chronicle* to reassure the
Reformers that many of the notices of objection served by the
Tories were bound to fail upon a technicality. He had to be
corrected, in alarm and great haste, the very next day, by James
Coppock, the Whig agent.[66] The *County Herald*, in calling upon
its readers to attend the revision courts, hit the nail on the head
when it said that by doing so they might serve themselves and
others in a hundred 'unexpected' ways,[67] rescuing valid votes
from vexatious objections, and also, as the *Surrey Standard*
pointed out, evading *bona fide* objections to their invalid
claims.[68]

An outraged public was not slow to make its own summary
of the position at the end of 1835. In the boroughs the law did
not even require the service of notices of objection. In the
counties, where service was required, it was not necessary to
state the grounds of objection. The electors whose votes were
objected to had no means of knowing in advance what docu-
ments they ought to take with them to the revising barrister's
court in order to substantiate their claims. Even if they were
fortunate enough to save their votes one year, there was no rule
against repeated objections, and they might still be called upon
to defend them again the next year and the year after that. With
a different revising barrister there might be different results. All
seemed arbitrary: the barristers 'constitute the law. They do not
represent it',[69] and according to their politics the newspapers
drew their own conclusions. The Tory *Western Luminary*
proclaimed that it was impossible to continue with the law as it
was — meaning the Reform Act — and urged a restriction of the
franchise.[70] The Radical *Manchester and Salford Advertiser*, on
the other hand, stigmatised the Reform Act as 'an Act to
enfranchise persons in order to take away their votes' and
argued that the thing to do was to sweep away all the
restrictions placed upon the franchise and advance to universal
suffrage, which would be much easier to administer.[71] The
Advertiser's near, and perhaps fortunately more influential,
neighbour, the *Manchester Guardian*, struggled to help its
readers keep their heads upon their shoulders. Many of the
points which were now troubling the revising barristers, it said,
were not new, and had vexed the sheriff's assessors before 1832.

Nobody could have expected everything to come right all at once and the keen contests of the present year had at least made it clear what the problems were.[72] One thing there was, however, upon which all shades of opinion were unanimous, and that was that in the next session of Parliament some attempt must be made to amend and to clarify the law. Why that amendment and clarification did not take place will appear in the next chapter.

4 The Parties Stand on Their Heads

The events of the 1835 registration, when, 'rather than yield the slightest advantage to the adversary', the franchised populations of whole parishes were 'immolated on the altar of party zeal',[1] convinced everyone that something must be done, and it was generally understood that a new Bill, based upon the experience of the original registration in 1832 and the three annual revisions of 1833, 1834 and 1835, would be introduced in the next session. Although extremist editors of the Tory press sought to exploit dissatisfaction with the registration system in order to discredit the Reform Act as a whole, moderate Conservatives welcomed the prospect of putting an end to abuses which lowered politics in the esteem of the public, and in theory at least it ought to have been easy to bring the parties to agreement. But even in the comparatively 'quiet' days of 1834 it must have been apparent that any new procedure for the registration of voters could not but affect the franchise; and in a period when the parties were still trying to count their gains and losses at the registration of 1835 it was inconceivable that any measure could be drafted which would not be thought to be framed for electoral advantage. Party begets party begets party, and the prospects for reform were not as bright as they seemed.

It is difficult to penetrate the fog of claim and counter-claim surrounding the parties' fortunes in the 1835 registration. The newspapers were partisan, and, as there were two ways of scoring, by adding to one's own voters and by striking off those on the other side, it was easy to slant the reporting of the revision. In a single constituency one side might have substan-

tiated more new claims and the other struck off more established voters, and both parties would then claim the victory, as
happened at Canterbury, where the Reformers celebrated with a
great 'blue' dinner and the Tories held a great 'red' one.[2]
Similarly, in a much more important constituency like the West
Riding it was possible for the *Leeds Intelligencer* to claim that
the Conservatives had struck off nearly 3000 claimants who,
'but for the Revising Court, would have swelled the ranks of the
Movement army',[3] and for the *Leeds Mercury* to reply, equally
plausibly, that the Reformers' majority would now be 1000
more than it had been at the last election.[4] At the national
level the effect of the revision was argued out in the columns
of the *Standard* and the *Morning Chronicle*. For the Tories
the *Standard* claimed that the results were 'everywhere
enormously in their favour. The Destructives have absolutely no
per contra to show'.[5] On the other side, the *Morning Chronicle*
rested its case largely upon the contention that, the Reformers
having neglected the registration in 1833 and 1834, the greater
part of the 'extraordinary increase' which had taken place in the
county constituency must be Liberal.[6]

Both parties professed themselves satisfied with their progress
at the registration, but there are indications that, more often
than not, the Tories had the better of it. The *Morning
Chronicle*'s case seemed to rely heavily upon gains at Bristol,
Colchester, Dover and Halifax,[7] and the somewhat muted tone
of the Liberal *County Herald*, which circulated in the counties
round London, suggests that, in this area at least, the Tories
were in fact doing better than the Reformers.[8] The *Surrey
Standard* arrogantly observed that the Destructives lacked the
sinews of war,[9] and this point was echoed as far away as
Lancashire, where the *Manchester Guardian* referred to the
Tories' *very* superior command of money'.[10] In the deep
countryside the *Herefordshire Journal* thought things had gone
the Conservatives' way throughout the county,[11] and to this
the *Hereford Times* could only reply that at all events they had
not gone the Conservatives' way at Ledbury.[12] Further
evidence leading in the same direction comes from the ever
increasing volume of complaints in the Liberal newspapers
about the renewal of intimidation. In 1832 there were many
counties where the landlords had relaxed their hold over their
tenants;[13] but in 1835 it was alleged that the cause of Lord

John Russell's defeat in South Devonshire was that 1500
farmers and tradesmen who had promised to vote for the
government had been obliged by the threat of eviction to poll
the other way.[14] In the boroughs, too, it was alleged that
tradesmen had been *'marked down*, and starvation inscribed
upon their doors, by wealthy Tories, clergymen, naval and
military officers and others',[15] but the Reformers were able to
sweep the board at the first elections for the new town councils
in December 1835, and when the new session of Parliament
opened in 1836 both parties had cause to fear the consequences
of a dissolution of Parliament, which would put both Whig
counties and Tory boroughs at risk.

It was in these circumstances that the Whigs attempted to
resolve the problems surrounding the registration. Their draft
Bill of 1836 included clauses to restrict the repetition of
objections year by year, and to empower the revising barristers
to award costs against vexatious objectors.[16] These proposals
were relatively uncontroversial, and, encouraged by their recep-
tion, Ministers went on to suggest, in the committee stage, a
much more fundamental overhaul of the whole system. The 160
revising barristers, it now appeared, had been a mistake. First,
there were too many of them; secondly, a successful lawyer
would not take on the work. The result was that a majority of
the revising barristers were young men, and therefore inexperi-
enced, while those who were not young were, by definition,
unsuccessful lawyers. Hence the confusion of contradictory
decisions and the tactless and provocative handling of claimants.
To replace them, the Whigs now proposed to appoint eleven
full-time, permanent and official revising barristers. The Chief
Revising Barrister would form a court of appeal (another
important innovation) from the decisions of the remainder, who
would be sent out on circuit to cover the entire electorate once
in the course of each year.[17] The annual registration battle
would thus take place constituency by constituency, and month
by month, and the country would be relieved from what
seemed to many to be an annual 'general election' (to be
followed by annual parliaments?) every 15 September to 25
October.

Hitherto the Conservative opposition had denounced the
existing registration system for its bad workmanship, and
expressed its willingness to co-operate in changing it. Now

Conservative reaction to the government's proposals centred upon the clause placing the appointment of the revising barristers in the hands of the Home Secretary (Lord John Russell). Peel objected to this, and argued explicitly and bluntly that there would be less danger of partiality if the choice were to be made by the Lord Chancellor.[18] What followed set the pattern for the barren politics of the Parliamentary stalemate of the later 1830s. Neither party wished to be saddled with the responsibility for a breakdown, and Lord John accordingly moved halfway, or more than halfway, to meet Peel's objection. He agreed that the first eleven full-time revising barristers should be named in the Bill and approved by Parliament, and he persuaded Sir William Follett (Tory, Exeter) to co-operate with Sir F. Pollock (Whig, Huntingdonshire) in their selection. He then announced the names, and conceded that future replacements were to be made by the Lord Chancellor of the day.[19] Thus far did he succeed in drawing the Tory party on towards a settlement, but the Bill would have clarified the position of the chapel trustees and guaranteed the franchise to any trustee who enjoyed complete discretion in the expenditure of the income from a trust. Conservative MPs did not agree with the *Manchester Guardian* that 'at the very least dissenting trustees are as intelligent and independent a body, and have quite as much stake in the country, as farm tenants at will':[20] the point was not negotiable, and Peel's lieutenants, Bonham, Sir Thomas Fremantle and Lord Granville Somerset, were therefore mobilised to raise renewed objections to the whole measure. The Whigs' Bill passed the House of Commons, but was then abandoned, since there was no point in proceeding with it in the Upper House.

The result was that at the registration of 1836 the Reformers lost heart, and the solicitors who formed the backbone of the Conservative party's organisation in every constituency showed more zeal than their Liberal counterparts, who took the lead even, in a number of places, in offering a truce. The newspaper press provides us with an interesting explanation why this should have been so. The Tories made no secret of their preference for a restricted franchise and a 'cleansed' constituency, and no taint of hypocrisy attached to them as they went about the unattractive aspects of the registration process. The Reformers, on the other hand, were at a double disadvantage when they stooped to the same tricks, because both the Tory and the Radical press pilloried them as the reducers of the franchise and the enemies of the people. Many Reformers were genuinely reluctant to sow 'the alarming crop of ill-will and hatred which must be looked for ... [when] agents ... prowl about, seeking any means ... for depriving their fellow subjects of the first ... right of citizenship'.[21] Little wonder, then, that at the end of the revision of 1836 the Conservative agent, Bonham, was able to assure Peel that he could look forward to a gain of fifty seats in England alone, if the Tories came back into office and dissolved Parliament.[22]

At some time in this period it dawned upon both parties that what was happening was not just that the Tories were winning the battle of the registration courts, but that the whole registration system operated in their favour. As the *Manchester and Salford Advertiser* put it, the Act of 1832 had given the Tories the key to the citadel.[23] A majority of the judges who appointed the revising barristers were anti-Whig, and the revising barristers themselves 'chuckle ... at the facilities given for cutting away votes, and at the power left them, by the impenetrable language of the act, to interpret it almost always in the sense of disfranchisement'.[24] This view was not confined to the Radical wing of the party, and in 1841 the Leader of the House of Commons said that the ordinary practice of courts of law 'is generally to restrict the franchise by technical definitions and distinctions'.[25] There was scope for men to differ in their estimates of the exact degree of partiality displayed by the revising barristers, but after five years experience there could be no doubt that, the more conditions claimants were required to satisfy and the more narrowly their claims to register were scrutinised, the more rejections there would be. The Tory *Surrey Standard* itself agreed that 'the entire working of the system is in favour of the Conservative party',[26] and the boasts of the Right thus corresponded exactly to the complaints of the Left. This was the point affairs had reached when William IV died, and the general election of 1837 confirmed the trend of the annual registrations and resulted in the capture by the Tories of another twenty-two English county seats. It then became certain that Peel's followers never would agree to changes in the registration system until they came into power and could make them in their own way. To that end they now addressed themselves. The general election of 1837 had left the Whig Ministry in a minority in Britain, dependent for its continued existence upon its majority in Ireland, where the Whigs had made a net gain of four seats and where the Whigs and the Repealers together now held seventy-one of the 105 seats.[27] For the remainder of the decade, therefore, the Tories concentrated their attention upon the state of affairs in Ireland, whose constituency stood between them and power.

The Act of Union with Ireland, which was passed in 1800 and came into force on 1 January 1801, brought 100 Irish MPs into the parliament of what was henceforth known as the United Kingdom of Great Britain and Ireland. In Ireland as in England, Wales and Scotland, there were county constituencies (thirty-two, with two Members each) and borough constituencies (thirty-four, with one Member each, except for Dublin and Cork, which had two each). In the counties there was at that time a large electorate recruited on a complicated three-tier franchise of £50 freeholders, £20 freeholders, and forty-shilling freeholders, the different levels supposedly marking different degrees of independence. The Irish boroughs were of two kinds. Ten of the large towns, headed by Dublin, Cork and Limerick, contained sizable constituencies, running into − or, in the case of Carrickfergus and Londonderry, approaching − four figures, while the remainder possessed very small ones indeed − the types being Belfast and Armagh, where the franchise was restricted to a sovereign (mayor) and twelve burgesses. The tiny boroughs were not exclusively Tory (in 1826 Lord John Russell was returned for Bandon Bridge, thirteen voters, at the instance of the Earl of Clare),[28] and Ulster rather than the small boroughs formed the secure basis of Tory, Orange and Protestant domination, which reached out still further into many of the larger boroughs through the creation of freemen, and into the counties through the power of the great landlords of the ascendancy.

Seven-eighths of the population of Ireland were Roman Catholic and in 1801 the position was that Catholics could vote at elections but might not be elected to Parliament or hold office. Not surprisingly, therefore, the demand for civic equality could never be suppressed, and in 1829 Wellington and Peel were obliged to pass the Act to emancipate the Catholics rather than fight a civil war. Simultaneously, in order to safeguard the ascendancy, they disfranchised the forty-shilling freeholders and raised the minimum qualification in the counties to £10, thus, at a stroke, reducing the electorate in the Irish counties from 216,871 to 39,772.[29]

In 1829 the Whig opposition accepted the disfranchisement for the sake of the greater good which was emancipation. But, when the Whigs came into power in 1830, and passed Reform Acts for England and Wales, and Scotland, it was natural that they should attempt to do something for Ireland too. In 1832 the representation of Ireland was increased from 100 to 105 MPs, and, running along the lines laid down by the English Reform Act, the Whigs provided both for the gradual extinction of freemen in the boroughs as existing life interests disappeared and for the introduction of a new £10 householder franchise, while both the borough and the county electorates were extended by the enfranchisement of £10 leaseholders.[30] These measures, which had the effect of creating something like a legitimate political life in many of the Irish boroughs, and of increasing the electorate in the counties to 58,931,[31] were the work of Stanley, a young Whig aristocrat who was later alleged to have denounced the extent of the disfranchisement in 1829,[32] and who was in 1832 the Chief Secretary for Ireland.

After 1832 the government of Ireland became the main bone of contention, first between the right and left wings of the Whig party, and then, after the right wing had been driven out by the left, between the Liberal majority in the House of Commons and the Tory and Orange majority in the House of Lords. The Reformers were determined to pursue a policy of equal-treatment-under-the-Union for Ireland, and to this end they were prepared to 'appropriate' (or confiscate) the excess revenues of the Established Church in Ireland and to ally with O'Connell and the Repeal party. The results were to drive Stanley himself, Emerson Tennent — Stanley's mentor upon Irish affairs — and Sir James Graham across the floor of the House (a severe loss in terms of experience and talent for future debates upon the registration), and to generate a sense of outrage among the Tories and of unease among some of the surviving Whigs at the association of English gentlemen with Irish demagogues. In these circumstances all the Reformers' attempts to legislate for Ireland between 1835 and 1837 were contemptuously blocked by the House of Lords, and the Ministry was obliged to attempt to achieve by executive action what it could not accomplish by legislation — a policy which held out a greater prospect of success in Ireland than it would have done in England. The Lord Lieutenant and the administration in Dublin Castle included Roman Catholics in the distribution of Crown patronage, found them situations in the police, and by-passed the Orange justices of the peace with the appointment of stipendiary magistrates. But it was of the essence of executive action, depending so largely upon the appointment of men of the right 'colour' to offices as they became vacant, that time was needed if it were to succeed. A strengthened executive followed by an early return of the Tories to power might leave the Irish worse off than they had been before, and after the general election of 1837 the position was, therefore, that the Whigs must remain in office long enough to make such an impact upon the government of Ireland that even a future Tory administration would be unable to turn the clock back.

The Irish Members themselves responded warmly to this policy, and in 1839—40 they supported Melbourne's government in the debates upon the education grant, Chartism, and even Canada (where the Repealers, at least, might have been expected to make common cause with the French rebels). Since it seemed to be impossible, once the Irish MPs reached Westminster, to split them from the Whigs, the Tories began increasingly to wonder whether they might not, after all, destroy them at source. Elections were now won and lost in the registration courts, and the Tories developed a 'lynx-eyed' vigilance in detecting the abuses of the Irish registration.[33]

The Irish system of registration was much older than the English one and reached back in origin to statutes (of the Irish parliament) of 1727 and 1795.[34] The system was overhauled in 1829 and again in 1832,[35] and the position now was that the £50 freeholders (many of whom were absentees) could register their votes at any superior Court of Record in Dublin or before any judge of assize,[36] but that lesser electors were obliged first to lodge a claim and then to attend quarter-sessions, where their claims were examined by the assistant barrister.[37] Under Irish law the successful claimant had always been accustomed to receive a certificate entitling him to vote, and the Act of 1832 left unchanged the procedure by which these certificates were valid and virtually unassailable for eight years.[38] Unlike the English system, the Irish one made provision for appeals, and disappointed claimants could appeal to the judges at assize. In cases where the issue at stake was the value of the property, the judge was then to have the assistance of a jury.[39]

The first fault fastened upon by critics of the Irish electoral system was the issue of octennial certificates. In the first place, the registered elector who had gone down in the world retained his vote until his certificate expired. In the second place, in a country where huge extended families answered to the same name and were not known in person to the agents of the ascendancy, registered electors who had died or left the district were easily impersonated by others, who presented their certificates. In the third place, although an elector was not required to make a new claim until his certificate expired, there was nothing to stop him making a new claim every year if he wanted to, and obtaining a new certificate each time. Incredible as it may seem, there was no procedure for cancelling old certificates, and towards the end of the decade it was alleged that in Belfast there were 6000 certificates in existence among a population where the qualified electorate did not exceed 2000, and that they passed from hand to hand like Exchequer bills.[40] Nobody could deny that this was an abuse, and in 1835, when equality under the Act of Union was the watchword of the day, and the Whigs were attempting to deal with the registration as with other Irish problems by assimilating Irish procedures to English ones, O'Connell himself denounced the evils of the quarterly registration and the octennial certificates, and asked rhetorically 'what reason there was that there should not be an annual revision of the registry in Ireland as in England?'[41]

The second fault in the Irish electoral system was that it led to disputes about the franchise. These turned upon the distinction between what was known as 'the solvent tenant test' and the concept of 'a beneficial interest'. The Catholic Emancipation Act of 1829 had restricted the franchise to the £10 freeholder, and, since the idea of a freeholder paying rent has died out, it may be as well to explain that in Ireland at this period a freeholder was frequently a tenant for life or for a succession of lives, and that many Irish freeholders held their land for life or for a succession of lives upon condition that they paid, every year, a certain (probably rather nominal) sum in rent. Accordingly the Act of 1829 required the claimant to swear that he possessed a freehold of the clear yearly value of £10 over and above all charges, 'and that a solvent and responsible Tenant could, as I verily believe, afford to pay for the same, as an additional Rent, fairly and without Collusion, the annual Sum of Ten Pounds, over and above all Rent to which I am liable in respect thereof . . . .'[42] It was commonly said that this oath turned a £10 franchise into a £20 one — that, before his name could be accepted onto the register, a man had to make £10 for himself and £10 which he could spare to his landlord.[43] This was approximately true, and a freeholder's claim to register developed into a contest between his friends, who swore that they would be willing to pay £10 a year more for his plot than he did, and his enemies, who took their oath that no man would be willing to pay £10 a year more for his plot than he did.[44]

The freeholder's oath under the Act of 1829 might almost have been designed to extract solicited testimonials to the benevolence of Irish landlords. Deplorable as this was, it did the freeholders little harm, because their rents were fixed by agreements which were enforceable in the courts, and there was scant danger of their rents being increased because they had had the temerity to claim their votes. But the freeholder's oath was obviously unsuitable for the leaseholders enfranchised under the Act of 1832, who would find that attempts to claim the franchise would lead automatically to swingeing increases in their rents when their leases ran out. Furthermore, in the case of the many tenants who held leases for terms of fourteen or even twenty years, and were accustomed to take out new leases every year, the effects of any enforced declarations that they could afford to pay more rent would be immediate. In their Act of 1832, therefore, the Whigs dropped the formula contained in the freeholder's oath appended to the Act of 1829 and substituted for it a declaration that the claimant enjoyed 'a beneficial interest' of £10 per annum in his holding.[45] There seems to have been genuine confusion in the House of Lords at the time as to the construction to be put upon this term. Orange and Conservative peers took fright because they supposed that anyone who conducted a business with an annual

turnover of £10 would be able to take his oath that his tenancy
was worth £10 to him. This would mean that every man who
held a cabin with an acre of ground, and every man who carried
on a trade in his house would lay claim to a place on the
register.[46] Stigmatising this as universal suffrage, the Archbishop of Armagh complained bitterly that the security held
out to the rule of Protestant wealth over Catholic numbers in
the disfranchisement of the forty-shilling freeholders was being
neutralised, in three short years, 'by the creation of a more
dangerous class of voters'.[47]

This was a misunderstanding, but, even after government
spokesmen had reassured the peers that in Ireland, as in
England, beneficial interest would be defined not in terms of
annual turnover, but in its more ordinary sense of profit (better
income?) after all expenses and charges had been met,[48] there
was still plenty of scope left for the parties and their agents to
disagree about the exact relationship in which the Acts of 1829
and 1832 stood to each other, and two main interpretations
arose. According to the Reformers the Act of 1832 had done
away with the solvent tenant test altogether, and freeholders,
like leaseholders, need only prove that they enjoyed a beneficial
interest or profit of £10 a year to make a claim to register. In
addition to enfranchising the leaseholders for the first time, the
Act of 1832 had, therefore, also opened the door to the
registration of a large number of extra freeholders. According to
the Tories the Act of 1832 had not repealed the solvent tenant
test contained in the Act of 1829, and the solvent tenant test
therefore remained the only legal way of assessing the extent of
a beneficial interest. It followed that the freeholder's oath now
applied both to freeholders and to leaseholders (for whom it
would be the kiss of death).

In 1832 a majority of the assistant barristers appear to have
interpreted the Act in a generous sense.[49] The result was that
the first register compiled under the Act contained enough
names to ensure that for the next eight years a majority of the
Irish MPs would incline towards O'Connell and the Whigs rather
than the Tories, and, when a rejected claimant lodged an appeal
in County Louth, and Chief Justice Bushe of the King's Bench
ruled in favour of the ordinary, wider interpretation of the term
'beneficial interest', it appeared that the Whigs had secured a
permanent advantage.[50] It was not for long: there were not

many appeals in Ireland, because rejected claimants preferred to wait and take their chance with the assistant barrister at the next quarter sessions, and in 1837 a report showed that in fourteen out of twenty-nine counties no appeal had ever yet been made.[51] However, the political parties encouraged appeals when they thought they might obtain a favourable definition of the law, and in 1832 Chief Justice Doherty of the Common Pleas and Chief Baron Joy of the Exchequer gave a ruling in County Longford, and in 1835 Doherty gave one in Queen's County, in favour of the solvent tenant test and the freeholder's oath contained in the Act of 1829, as being the only method of establishing the extent of a beneficial interest under the Act of 1832.[52]

The assistant barristers were expected to conform to the decisions of the judges, and since the judges were divided, the interpretation of the Irish franchise became a matter of hazard. Accordingly, when they came back into power in 1835, the Reformers gave high priority to a Bill to clarify Irish electoral law.[53] Linking the two main problems, they proposed to replace the quarterly registration with an annual one, to prohibit the issue of certificates, and to enact the generous interpretation of the term beneficial interest. The Tories welcomed the proposal to put an end to the certificates, but expressed fear that the clause defining the franchise had been introduced by some master hand for some master purpose.[54] The Whigs' Irish Registration Bill of 1835, therefore, came to nothing, and a similar Bill the next year met the same fate.

In 1837 the whole question of the Irish registration became much more acute. It was the practice of the twelve Irish judges, when they were at odds among themselves, to meet and come to a decision, by a majority if need be, which was subsequently accepted even by the dissentients, and the next time the question of the solvent tenant test came before Chief Justice Bushe, upon Matthew Glennon's appeal to the spring assizes for 1837 in County Cavan, he decided to bring the issue to a head. Contrary to his own opinion, he directed the jury to try the case according to the solvent tenant test, and then referred to the whole body of the Irish judges the question whether the jury had upon this occasion been correctly charged.[55]

The case was argued before the twelve judges of Ireland on 27 and 31 May, and upon 13 June 1837 judgement was delivered. Chief Justice Bushe, Mr Justice Burton and Mr Justice Crampton, of what was still for another week (until the death of William IV) to be the Court of *King's* Bench, held that, while a jury might, at its discretion, employ the solvent tenant test in order to establish the extent of a beneficial interest, it ought not to be given an exclusive instruction to do so, and that the charge administered to the jury upon this occasion was incorrect. Mr Justice Perrin of the King's Bench and Baron Richards of the Exchequer went further, and argued that the solvent tenant test ought never to have been used at all. But the four judges of the Common Pleas, Chief Justice Doherty, Mr Justice Johnson, Mr Justice Moore and Mr Justice Torrens, and three out of the four barons of the Exchequer, Chief Baron Joy, Baron Foster, and Baron Pennefather, all seven of whom had either been appointed before 1830 or in the early days of Grey's administration,[56] held that the solvent tenant test was the only legal way of establishing the extent of a beneficial interest and that the charge given to the jury had been correct. The question then arising as to whether the decision in Matthew Glennon's case should stand, Chief Justice Bushe, Mr Justice Burton and Mr Justice Crampton surrendered their opinions and joined forces with the seven, leaving Mr Justice Perrin and Baron Richards, both appointed by the Whigs after the retirement of Grey, in a minority of two to ten.

In the meantime the Tories in Parliament had not been idle, and in 1837 they had secured the appointment of a Select Committee of the House of Commons to inquire into the existence of fictitious voters in Ireland. The evidence published by this committee[57] was already beginning to impress the general public with the evils of the octennial certificates, when the general election of 1837 left the Whig Ministry entirely dependent, for its continued existence, upon the votes of a majority of the Irish MPs. The extraordinary drama of the next few years has never yet received the attention it deserves. The Whigs were engaged upon a crusade to secure justice for Ireland, but the suspicion was growing, with every fresh inquiry into the recent elections, that the life of the Ministry now hung by a thread of fictitious votes polled through the misuse of the octennial certificates.

Everything now went against the Ministry. The new Parliament appointed a second committee of inquiry into fictitious votes,[58] and, when the two out-and-out Whig Judges, Perrin and Richards, defied the opinion of the majority of their colleagues, and continued to decide registration appeals without reference to the solvent tenant test, Chief Justice Bushe felt obliged to write on 8 February 1838, to Lord Denman, the senior English judge, to obtain a ruling that the opinion of a majority of the judges ought to be binding upon the remainder – else were the law uncertain.[59] This meant that the Tories themselves would no longer need to legislate in order to secure the narrow franchise they preferred. Treating the franchise as a settled question, they were able thereafter to concentrate upon the abuse of the certificates, and had, in any case, only to wait until the majority of octennial certificates, which had never yet been renewed, ran out in November 1840 to achieve a substantial reduction in the overall numbers of the Irish electorate. The Whigs, on the other hand, dare not legislate to abolish the certificates without securing a wider definition of the franchise, and could not pass any legislation of which the House of Lords disapproved. Unable to legislate, their one remaining hope lay in hanging on to power long enough to secure a majority among the judges. They would never be permitted to pass a new Act defining the franchise on their own terms, but they might yet remain in charge of affairs long enough to secure their own interpretation of the Act of 1832. In the meantime they were reduced to defending the eight-year certificates and the fictitious votes which flowed from them. It was scarcely a dignified situation for the purists in politics to find themselves in. In 1835 and 1836 they had offered to abolish the certificates:[60] now, in their Irish registration Bill of 1838 they were moving towards their retention,[61] and argued that further experience with the system of annual revision in England had shown that there, too, an elector ought to be able to establish his vote for more than one year at a time.[62] Finally, in 1839, when W. S. O'Brien, a moderate Irish MP, attempted to secure a compromise between the parties, O'Connell abruptly told him that any cleansing of the constituency would eliminate the Reformers' majority, and persuaded him to leave ill alone.[63]

To a committed Whig like Lord John Russell the end justified the means, and for a time it may almost have seemed that the Whigs would succeed. In 1838 Chief Baron Joy died and was replaced by Woulfe (and in due course by Brady), and in 1839

Mr Justice Moore of the Court of Common Pleas died and was replaced by Ball. One judge on the Queen's Bench, one in the Common Pleas, and two barons of the Exchequer would then have been willing to give the ruling sought by the government, that the solvent tenant test ought never to be employed at all. But these four were scarcely in a position to combine with the three judges of the Queen's Bench who held that the solvent tenant test was one of several which a jury might employ at its discretion, in order to overwhelm the three judges of the Common Pleas and the two barons who still held that the solvent tenant test was the only valid test. In 1840 the Whigs were not yet in a position to establish their own interpretation of the law, but they had narrowed the gap, and for their part the Tories, as they prepared to launch an attack upon the certificate system, which they were bound to do — if it were to be done at all — in the session before so many certificates expired, must have cast anxious glances at the healths of 'their' judges upon the Irish bench.

Stanley's Irish Registration Bill of 1840 was extremely skilfully drafted and presented. Speaking as though he were still Chief Secretary for Ireland, Stanley thanked the judges for having resolved the uncertainties surrounding the franchises introduced in 1832, and argued that it remained only to tidy up the Irish registration procedures which Grey's government had deliberately reserved for future consideration when more was known about the working of the annual registration system in England. Now that experience had proved the English system a success, Stanley put himself forward as offering, if the government could not find time to do it, to complete his own work of 1830—3 by assimilating Irish procedures to English ones as had been intended all along, and as the Whigs themselves were always saying they wished to do in other fields. In place of the quarterly registration and the eight-year certificates he proposed to adopt the English county system, under which a new list would be drawn up every year. No certificates would be issued, and the scope of the existing procedure for appeals, which had no counterpart in England but which Stanley thought ought to be adopted there, would be extended in order to allow unsuccessful objectors to lodge appeals against successful claimants.[64]

It is not easy to gauge the potential effects of Stanley's Bill.

The Whigs and Irish argued that, had it been passed, the action of organised party would have ensured that objections were lodged with the judges on appeal, sitting anything up to fifty miles away from an elector's home, and that the sequence of claim and appeal, claim and appeal, continuing year by year, would have deterred many, even of those who were qualified, from attempting to secure places on the register.[65] This might have been the case, but the action of organised party would not have been confined to one side; the Whigs and the Irish would not have been the only ones to lose from the termination of the certificate system; and Sir William Somerville was almost certainly exaggerating when he alleged that the effect of Stanley's Bill would have been to reduce the electorate to the point where the Reformers would not hold more than twenty out of the 105 seats.[66] The experience of the two general elections held under the restricted franchise of 1829, in 1830 and 1831, does not suggest that the consequences would have been as sweeping as that. But it was true that O'Connell's Irish and the Whigs, as the majority parties, had more to lose than the Tories, and that a small change in the relative strengths of the parties in Ireland would result in the loss of the Melbourne Ministry's majority in the House of Commons. Everyone knew what was at stake: 'The Irish Members obstructed the noble Lord's [Stanley's] attainment of office, therefore they were to be removed at any cost';[67] and the problem for the Whigs was that many of Stanley's clauses were taken almost verbatim either from the Whig Bills of 1835 and 1836 or from O'Brien's proposals of 1839. The truth was, as one Tory expressed it, that Ministers had since discovered that 'the removal of these abuses would operate to the prejudice of their own party interests'.[68] However vehemently Ministers might argue, pointing to Stanley, and to Emerson Tennent, who had once been a Radical and a Repealer, that they were not the only ones to have changed their minds,[69] and however forceful their case for the abolition of the solvent tenant test, the fact remained that, in taking up the position that they would never agree to the abolition of the certificates until the Tories accepted an enlarged franchise, Ministers were for the first time explicitly committing themselves to the preservation of an acknowledged abuse.

Year by year since the Whigs joined the Radicals and the Irish in 1835, the alliance had endured. The Radicals might become disaffected, bring in motions of their own about the secret ballot, and vote against the government on Jamaica. But upon every issue of Irish policy, the appropriation of the surplus revenues of the Irish church, the tithes, the municipal corporations, and the general conduct of Mulgrave's administration, the Whigs, Radicals and Irish had presented a solid front against the common enemy.

Events were to show that the Tories had now, at last, discovered an Irish issue which would split the Whig party. Stanley's Bill was opposed by Ministers, but it passed its second reading on 26 March by 250 votes to 234. Thereafter the government suffered four more defeats, including two major ones on 18 May (by 281 to 262) and 20 May (by 301 to 298), before it was at last able to secure a majority upon an amendment on 19 June, by 296 votes to 289. It was defeated again on 26 June before Stanley's Bill disappeared into the expiring sands of the session, and even this long list of defeats does not complete the tale of the government's discomfiture, because, in April, knowing that every vote was vital, Ministers delayed issuing the writ for the by-election at Ludlow, where they expected to be defeated, and in debates raised upon this proceeding they were defeated no fewer than seven times, on 11 and 12 May.

A Liberal Ministry must always be liable to defections on both flanks, by the Radicals if it is not active enough, and by the Whigs with Tory feelings if it is too active, and after 1837 Melbourne's Ministry suffered successively, first from Lord John Russell's declaration as to the Finality of the Reform Act, which offended the Radicals, and then, in 1839, after the Bedchamber Crisis, from its *rapprochement* with the Radicals and its decision to make both the secret ballot and the repeal of the Corn Laws open questions.[70] The consequence was that, by the time the vote was taken upon the Tory motion of no confidence at the beginning of the session in 1840, two former Whigs, Harcourt (Oxfordshire) and Vernon Harcourt (East Retford) had already deserted to the Tories, while two Radicals, Fielden (Oldham) and Turner (Blackburn), and one more Whig with Tory feelings, Calcraft (Wareham), were prepared to vote against the Ministry. Fielden, the factory reformer, was known as 'the self-acting mule' and it seems likely that neither his vote nor Turner's evinced a settled determination to destroy the

Ministry. In the debates upon Stanley's Bill which followed, Fielden cast no further votes against the government, though he abstained twice, while Turner evidently returned to the fold (paired once). Much more serious for the government was the revolt at the right-hand end of the spectrum. The two Harcourts were brothers, sons of an Archbishop of York, who had been brought up as Grenvillite Whigs. Their defections were permanent, and like Calcraft's were malignant. For the remainder of the session all three voted upon every issue with the Tory party. To these malignants it seems safe to add Walter Long (North Wiltshire) and Goring (Shoreham), both of whom abstained in the motion of no confidence, but voted against the government on all issues thereafter, and Tomline (Sudbury), who came in as a Whig at a by-election in June 1840, but lost no time in voting with the Tories.

In addition to the malignants, the debates upon Stanley's Irish registration Bill produced a new crop of rebels who voted against the government upon this one issue. Among the Radicals, Ainsworth (Bolton) voted against the government four times and made no secret of his reasons for doing so. Ainsworth had served upon two Select Committees of Inquiry into Irish elections,[71] and had become so indignant at the revelation of Irish electoral malpractices that he wholeheartedly approved of Stanley's proposal to abolish certificates and to institute an annual registration.[72] On the other flank, among the Whigs with Tory feelings, no one spoke out so plainly as Ainsworth, but Stanley's Bill brought new rebellions from Bassett (who was returned at a by-election for Helston in March — three votes against the Ministry and one absence), Benett (South Wiltshire — four absences and one vote against), Ingham (South Shields — five votes against), and Ponsonby (Poole — one vote against, one absence and one pair). Finally, the rebels were joined by two ex-Ministers, who had resigned in pique when Melbourne reconstructed the Ministry in August 1839; Howick (North Northumberland — two votes against and one absence) and Wood (Halifax — one vote against and one absence), who voted with the Ministry against giving Stanley's Bill a second reading, but subsequently thought that the House of Commons ought, for the sake of its public character, to proceed with the measure.[73] In an exquisite revenge upon their old colleagues, they then changed sides and voted against the government on

20 May, when their two votes made all the difference between a victory and a defeat.

To these rebels who actually voted against their own side, we must now add the much larger number of defectors who abstained. Fifty-three Reformers absented themselves on 26 March, sixty-two on 18 May, fourteen even on 20 May, which was regarded as the crucial division, nine on 19 June, when the government won, and sixteen on 26 June. The Tory record presents a remarkable contrast. On 26 March no more than nineteen Tories were absent, and on 19 June and 26 June not one was missing. Stanley praised his friends by saying that, in June 1840, in an unprecedented display of zeal for the public welfare, 300 gentlemen attended Parliament for three weeks without a defaulter.[74] Or, as O'Connell bitterly observed, 'Not one of the Tories is absent . . . nothing keeps them away when Ireland is to be injured.'[75] One can without hesitation assent to Peel's view that the second reading of Stanley's Bill was carried by the abstention of Liberal Members,[76] and, if we are to pay attention to the volume of complaint which appeared in the Liberal press at this period as to the practice of pairing,[77] it looks as though the defections may have spread even wider than this. Of course, we must be cautious about the pairs, for, however much one may suspect that a man who pairs is disaffected, it is impossible to be certain, and the man who pairs several times may be suffering from a serious illness, while the man who pairs once may not even have had a cold. But the fact remains that, upon the five major votes upon Stanley's Bill, no fewer than sixty-eight Reformers (apart from the malignants who voted against the government on every issue, and the rebels who voted against the government on this issue) were absent twice, or absent once and paired once, or paired twice. Even after discarding all those who were known to be ill, and all those whose reasons defy categorisation — like Campbell (Argyll), who refused to vote until he was offered a peerage[78] — it seems safe to suppose that abstention on this scale was not the result of mere carelessness, and we can find an explanation for it in the actions of Peel and Stanley, who addressed their speeches to what *they* called the 'independent' Members of the House of Commons,[79] *The Times* called the Gentlemen of England,[80] and Morpeth called a new species of game.[81] What Stanley said, in effect, was, 'O'Connell is not a gentleman, it never was very agreeable to your feelings when your leaders allied with him; you know, now, that many of his supporters have been returned to the House of Commons by fictitious votes: your feelings tell you not to vote with O'Connell, and your consciences tell you to vote for me.' Stanley was intimately acquainted with the views of the men he was addressing, and we come close to the essence of the whole episode when we recall that on 26 March, when O'Connell unwisely sneered at Stanley for neglecting his mother in law's funeral in order to attend the House,[82] the gentlemen of England were so outraged that Sir C. Lemon (West Cornwall) and Sir G. T. Staunton (Portsmouth) immediately walked out of the Chamber and two more votes were lost.[83]

Strange as it may seem, nowhere were the gentlemen of England more conspicuous than in Ireland itself, and one of the many embarrassments Ministers suffered was that the voting record of their Irish supporters was almost as bad as that of their English ones. Seven Irish supporters abstained on 26 March and fourteen more were paired, twelve were absent or paired on 18 May, seven were absent and two paired on 20 May, one was absent on 19 June, and three were absent on 26 June. The attendance of the Irish Members, like that of the remainder, improved during the session, but the fact that seventeen of its Irish supporters absconded at one time or another was a dispiriting thing for a government desperately trying to keep up the electorate in Ireland. Ministers were forced to recognise, however, that many Irish Whigs, like Sir Ralph Howard (County Wicklow — four abstentions), shared Stanley's views, and resented every effort O'Connell made to dictate to them how they should vote.

Upon this one issue a significant number of Reformers were not prepared to vote with their party right or wrong, and were willing, when the Ministry appeared to be committed to the defence of a gross abuse, to defy the party whip and to run the risk of the angry accusations which were bound to follow. The *Morning Chronicle* appealed to Liberal constituencies to teach their representatives not to absent themselves from their posts,[84] the *Manchester Guardian* wanted Fielden to be shown the displeasure of his constituents,[85] and the town council of Bolton actually sent a memorial to Ainsworth rebuking him for his conduct.[86] In Ireland, too, the *Dublin Evening Post* took up the cry, and at one time or another appeals were made to the constituents of Brabazon (County Dublin — three abstentions), Butler (County Kilkenny — one pair), Fitzgibbon (County Limerick — five abstentions), Howard (see above), and Macnamara (County Clare — one abstention), to remind their representatives whose representatives they were.[87] Butler subsequently voted with the government, and Macnamara was never absent again, but, in England, Ainsworth had the courage to justify himself,[88] and in general the intervention of the press appears to have strengthened the resolve of the delinquents.

In the meantime Ministers, who were unable to defeat Stanley's Bill outright, were obliged to counter it by inverting Stanley's arguments and announcing their intention of bringing in measures of their own. Teasing the Whigs for their policy of equality under the Union, Stanley had expressed his anxious desire to assimilate the Irish system of registration to the English one.[89] To this the Irish Members could at least reply that if Stanley was so concerned for electoral purity he ought to set his own house in order first. Were there no fictitious votes recorded at elections in England? Was there not universal complaint in England against a system which produced an annual 'election' rather than an annual revision?[90] As O'Connell put it: when in 1832 Stanley

> was asked to give the same system of registration to Ireland as had been established in England, his answer was brief but distinct: 'I cannot consent to introduce the English system of registration into Ireland as long as doubts exist as to whether it will work well in England'. The noble Lord had now found out that the system worked badly in England, and thereupon he proposed to introduce it into Ireland. Oh! if it had worked well in England, it would have been long enough before Ireland got it. But it had worked for evil, and therefore Ireland was to have it.[91]

In order to meet their own and O'Connell's wishes, Ministers then announced that they would bring in three Bills, to settle the Irish franchise, to reform the Irish registration system, and to amend the registration system in England and Wales. The first set out the point the Whigs must insist upon — the explicit rejection of the solvent tenant test.[92] Only when this was accepted would the government proceed, in its second Bill, to extinguish the eight-year certificates, year by year over an eight-year period.[93] In their third Bill,[94] Ministers addressed themselves to the problems of the registration in England, which now appeared of substance to them, but not to their opponents. Following along the path marked out by their Bill of 1836, they now proposed to appoint a body of fifteen revising barristers, twelve of whom would be sent out on circuit and three of whom would constitute a court of appeal. In order to continue the assimilation of Irish to English practice, they next proposed, in a change of tactics, to take appeals in Ireland away from the judges and send them to a tribunal of revising barristers.[95] Both England and Ireland would then have a 'professional' court of appeal, in both countries costs would be awarded against frivolous and vexatious objectors, and in both countries a man against whom an objection had been lodged, and whose case had been heard, would enter a new category of 'established' voters whose cases could not be re-opened except upon new grounds.

Finally, with their strongholds in the English boroughs in mind, the Whigs could not resist crossing the borderline which separated the registration from the franchise, and they announced their intention of doing away with the requirement that a £10 householder should have paid his assessed taxes, and of allowing the £10 householder who had moved house since the last registration to retain his vote.[96] Whatever the merits of these proposals, little more than academic interest attached to them at the time. The government's three Bills were spoiling devices, intended to secure delay until the next session, when, unless anything turned up during the recess, the whole question would, inevitably, have to be taken up again.

Before the new session opened in 1841, it must have become apparent to everyone that the Whigs' time was up. Only one more Irish judge had died, and as he was a Whig one, no further change had taken place in the overall composition of the Irish bench. In England the by-elections were going the Tories' way, and in Ireland the expiry of the original certificates granted under the Reform Act of 1832 had resulted in a startling drop in the numbers of the electorate. The county constituency, which had risen to 99,157 in 1839, had now fallen back to 57,104, and the number of registered electors in the boroughs, which had reached a peak of 55,530 in 1839, had dropped to 39,772.[9][7] After eight years in which it had not been possible to strike names off the lists, the registers had become swollen, and statistically almost valueless. A drop in the overall numbers was to be expected, and, without knowing how many persons whose names had been placed upon the original registers in November 1832 had since re-registered, it is impossible to form an exact impression of the extent of the disfranchisement repesented by these figures. But the point to fasten onto is that, after a period of eight years in which the number of registered electors in the counties might have been expected to increase, it was in fact now nearly 2000 lower than it had been immediately after the passage of the Reform Act. That was a measure of the success of the judges who had held to the solvent tenant test, and, that being so, the Whigs must now amend the Irish constituency or perish. In order to counter Stanley's new Irish Registration Bill of 1841, the Whigs, as Stanley himself recognised, would have to attempt to pass a new Irish Reform Act.[9][8]

This was not quite as hopeless a task as it might have appeared. Granted that Peel's return to power was now inevitable, Peel himself might possibly prefer to have the Irish registration issue out of the way before he took over. The Whigs' Registration Bill for England was almost identical with that of the year before,[9][9] but in their Irish Bill Ministers seized the opportunity to place the whole argument upon new ground,[100] and there seems to be no reason to doubt that in this manner they were making a serious attempt to reach a settlement, if Peel himself would have the good sense to grasp it. Both sides recognised that the great problem in Ireland was to find a true test of value. The Ministry could not return to the solvent tenant test of 1829, and the Act of 1832 had been emasculated by the judges. But there did, at last, appear to be a way out of the difficulty, for in 1838 Parliament had agreed to extend the English poor-law system to Ireland, and the first valuations for rating had now been completed. Here was a test which might be adopted as the basis of a new franchise: it contained a built-in check against fraud, for no man would demand a vote who lacked the means to pay the rates, and its adoption had, moreover, been suggested three years earlier, by Mr Fosbery, an assistant barrister with Tory prejudices, to the fictitious-votes committee.[101]

It remained to set a value which would create a 'real' constituency at least as large as that intended by the Whigs when they had passed the Act of 1832. Ministers selected a low figure of £5 rating, which they were presumably prepared to see amended in committee, and, in order to reassure the timid, combined it with the requirement of a fourteen-year lease.[102] This time Ministers managed to make their case for a reform of the Irish franchise intelligible, and this time every resource which friendship and party ties could suggest was employed to secure a majority for the second reading. Among the defaulters of 1840 four malignants, Calcraft, Goring, Harcourt and Long, and one rebel, Benett, remained implacable, and continued to vote with the Tories upon every issue. But two other malignants, Tomline and Vernon Harcourt, abstained, and one rebel, Ingham, paired. Among the English constituencies, one rebel upon the motion of no-confidence, Fielden, three rebels upon Stanley's Irish Registration Bill, Bassett, Howick and Wood, and at least seven contumelious defectors upon Stanley's Bill, Cayley, Fazakerley, G. J. Heathcote and Sir G. Heathcote, General Johnstone, Sir C. Lemon and Sir G. T. Staunton, actually returned to the fold and voted with the government. The Irish, too, achieved a better attendance, though Butler paired, and Sir Ralph Howard and Fitzgibbon both continued to abstain.

The government's Bill passed its second reading by a vote of 299 to 294. In view of what had happened the year before, this was no mean achievement, but it was obvious that a majority of five would be too small to carry the measure through the committee stage, when waverers like the two Heathcotes, for example, had voted for the second reading upon the explicit understanding that they would be free to object to the £5 rating at a later stage.[103] In order to obtain a settlement Ministers were prepared to accept an amendment substituting £8 for £5,[104] but the Bill then became entangled in one of Ireland's many great social problems, which was the attitude of landlords towards leases, and was caught in a cross-fire between those who feared that landlords would grant none, and those who feared that they would divide their holdings in order to manufacture them. Both groups feared the effect upon Irish politics, and upon the economy. These were problems that could not simply be brushed aside. Ebrington, the Lord Lieutenant, was worried lest the necessity for a lease would leave the future expansion and contraction of the constituency at the mercy of the landlords,[105] and, in one of those curious twists of Irish politics which occasionally bring extremes together, a number of the Whigs' Irish supporters made it clear that they, like the Tories, would prefer a simple occupation franchise. To the Irish this would have the advantage of producing a large electorate, to the Tories a potentially dependent one. Everything would then depend upon the extent to which the landlords could coerce the occupiers, or the occupiers, organised in secret societies, could terrorise their landlords. The proposal was a recipe for civil war, and it was one which no government could accept, but it was taken up by Howick and Wood, who somehow believed that they, in their turn, could mediate between the parties, and in two votes upon 26 and 29 April the government was defeated by 291 votes to 270, and by 300 votes to 289. Upon these two occasions, Bassett, Cayley, Fielden, the two Heathcotes, General Johnstone, Sir C. Lemon and Tomline, in addition to Howick and Wood, rebelled against their own party, and were joined by Dundas (York), and by two Irish Members, Cave (County Tipperary) and Corbally (County Meath). The Whigs were not to be allowed to pass a new reform or registration Bill for Ireland, and in due course, after the ministry had been defeated by one vote upon a motion of no confidence, the results in Ireland of the general election of 1841 confirmed the Reformers' worst fears. O'Connell's party lost fourteen seats, and was reduced to a rump of eighteen, and, although the Whigs saved some seats from the enemy, the Tories captured six Irish seats. For over six years O'Connell had used his authority as the head of the Repeal party to eschew violence in favour of constitutional methods within the framework of the Act of Union. Not even in alliance with the British government, however, had he been able to prevent a majority of the Irish judges interpreting the Act of 1832 in terms of the Act of 1829, and all he now had to show as the reward for his policy was a depleted following. He was left with no alternative but to return to extra-Parliamentary agitation if he were not to lose control of the Irish movement to younger and wilder men.

The Whigs, even more than O'Connell, it can be argued, were the real losers from the battle over the Irish registration. Upon the fundamental point, they had a good case, for it was indeed against public policy for the judges to interpret the beneficial-interest clauses of the Reform Act of 1832 in terms of the responsible and solvent tenant test contained in the Catholic Emancipation Act of 1829. But the issue was not one upon which Melbourne and Russell could hope to dissolve with any prospect of success in the English, Welsh and Scots constituencies; and, in meeting Stanley's Bill, they described a U-turn and ended up by arguing in favour of sin. In the debates upon Stanley's Bill, the Irishry of the Melbourne Ministry, or, as *The Times* said, 'its vital principle, that in which its whole being was framed, the milk which nourished it, the cradle wherein it was rocked, the garb which clothed it',[106] was exposed. Nemesis overtook Melbourne and Russell when a weakened Ministry was compelled to lead an embarrassed party into the general election of 1841, and their opponents were returned to power with an overall majority of over eighty.

5 The Tremendous Engine

Following his return to power in 1841, Peel no longer regarded the registration of voters in Ireland as a matter of great urgency. Why should he? The period of six years in which the ascendancy had felt itself threatened by the regime in Dublin Castle was over, and appointments to the Irish executive were now in his hands. With the death of Chief Justice Bushe in 1841, and the successive promotion to the bench of Blackburne, Lefroy and Jackson, the last two of whom had taken prominent parts in the debates upon Stanley's Registration Bill in 1840, the Irish franchise could safely be left to the Irish judges. The abuses of the certificate system, which had been pronounced intolerable so long as the Whigs were in office, were now lightly borne, and Ministers preferred to re-model the system of registration in England before attempting to assimilate the system in Ireland to it.

In England and Wales it was the Conservatives who had been able to exploit the deficiencies of the Act of 1832. The registration was known to be in their favour, and had acted, as Peel said, as 'a check . . . upon the efficiency and influence' of the Whig government, which met them upon 'every day and at every hour'.[1] But the feeling against the Act was universal, and now that Peel possessed the power it was time to amend it in his own way. He entrusted the task to Sir James Graham, who had previously drafted the registration clauses of the Act of 1832 which were now to be repealed. Graham was not the man to delay: he brought in a Bill in 1842,[2] and, when that failed for want of time, returned to the subject the next year, and passed the Act[3] which was to remain the basis of the registration law until 1918.[4]

Casting himself in the role of a man who has gained from experience, Graham made the overseers and the party agents the scapegoats for the unpopularity of his former measure. Upon many occasions the overseers had neglected to prepare the lists, while the zeal of parties had led both to frivolous claims and to vexatious and repeated objections. Henceforth the annual procedure was to be set in motion by the clerks of the peace and the town clerks, who were to call the attention of the overseers to their duties,[5] and henceforth the revising barristers were to have the power to penalise negligent overseers, and to award costs against persons making frivolous claims and vexatious objections.[6] Persons making objections in the boroughs were to be compelled to serve notice,[7] but by a striking omission neither they nor objectors in the counties, who were already compelled to serve notice, were to be required to give any indication of the grounds of their objections. In order to reduce disputes about the service of notices of objection, these might in future, as some revising barristers already permitted, be sent through the post, in which case the receipt of the postmaster who accepted the letter was to be taken as conclusive proof of delivery.[8]

The passage of time since 1832 had done something to bring the revising barristers to a common interpretation of the law, because a revising barrister who happened to go wrong 'was sure of not being dealt with very lightly . . . by his legal companions when he rejoined them at the Sessions, at the circuit table, [and] in Westminster Hall'.[9] But public disquiet at the capriciousness and at the absolute power of the revising barristers was still formidable, and the Act of 1843 therefore provided for appeals on points of law to be taken, at the discretion of the revising barristers, by both disappointed claimants and disappointed objectors, to the judges of the Court of Common Pleas.[10] This was long overdue, for, even if the existence of a court of appeal is not in itself essential to the concept of justice, the decisions of the court, unlike the proceedings of the revising barristers, would be certain to find their way into the Law Reports, and would help to bring the revising barristers to a conformity of opinion. The combined effect of all these measures, Graham thought, would be to reduce the number of cases brought before the revision courts and to expedite the determination of the remainder. Accordingly the number of revising barristers in England and Wales was to be reduced drastically, from 160 to eighty-five,[11] and, in order to allow the survivors a little more time to complete their tasks, the revision was henceforth to be completed by 31 October and the new registers were to come into force a month later, on 1 December in each year.[12]

Graham's Bill was intended to overhaul the registration machinery from bottom to top. Inattentive overseers, officious party agents, and slipshod and overbearing revising barristers were all put under restraint. Thus far the Bill appeared to have taken the measure of the problem, and thus far its provisions were not contentious. But there were other clauses in it which came to be seen in a different light. The politics of the 1830s had developed, in the eyes of contemporaries, into a struggle between the £50 tenants at will, who were regarded as the garrisons of the Tory strongholds in the shires, and the £10 householders, who formed the rank and file of the Reformers' citadels in the medium-sized and large towns. The Reformers naturally attributed the Tory success in the general election of 1841 to the systematic recruitment of the tenants at will. The Conservatives, with their fingers on the pulses of the county constituencies, were in a position to know better. The fact was that, ever since the heady days of 1835, the number of tenants at will registered in England had remained almost stationary, and between 1839 and 1842 had risen by only 2229, from 99,886 to 102,115.[13] In Tory eyes, at least, the explanation was not far to seek. The Act of 1832 had left the £50 tenants at will at a disadvantage, compared to the £10 householders, in two ways: the £10 householder was permitted to qualify in respect of the successive occupation of different houses, and joint occupants of houses in the boroughs were entitled to come onto the register provided their shares, if the property were divided, would come to £10 each.[14] There could be no fair-minded ground of complaint when the government proposed to allow the occupiers in the counties to qualify in respect of the successive occupation of different properties, and to permit joint occupiers to qualify provided their shares of the rent, if the property were divided, would come to £50 each.[15] But the tenants at will were an emotive subject, and opponents who thought that they ought never to have been enfranchised were

not likely to look kindly upon any provision which would add
to their numbers.

Having raised the occupants in the counties to the level of
those in the towns by allowing them to qualify in respect of
successive tenancies, Graham went on to abolish that part of the
oath tendered to voters at the polls which required them to
swear that they still possessed or occupied the same properties
in respect of which they had qualified. In both counties and
boroughs this had proved an irritant, and in the latter it had
produced the anomaly that a man might qualify to register in
respect of successive occupations, but, having qualified and seen
his name placed on the register, would then, if he moved house
again, find himself unable to vote until the next registration
season came round and he qualified again. Graham did not wish
to see this anomaly extended to the counties, and he therefore
provided that in future the elector presenting himself at the
polls need only swear that he was the person A.B. mentioned on
the register and that he had not already voted upon this
occasion.[16] The change would benefit the Reformers in the
towns at least as much as the Tories in the counties, but the
manner in which it was made left the impression that Peel's
administration would not attend to a grievance unless it
affected the £50 tenants at will — so suspicious had the parties
become of each other's motives.

It was one thing for Peel's Ministry to amend the law in such
a way as to add to the number of its own supporters. It was
another to change it in order to strike off opponents such as the
chapel trustees. Generally speaking, the revising barristers had
from the first been unfavourable to the claims of the chapel
trustees, as we have seen, and party agents had since subjected
them to a continuous war of attrition, with the result that in
North Warwickshire, for example, the fifty chapel trustees
placed upon the register in 1835 had been reduced to twenty-
six in 1836 and to nine in 1841. But the very notion of a
trustee of a Dissenting chapel securing a right to vote still
rankled with the Conservatives, and Graham determined, therefore, to enact the most restrictive possible interpretation[17] of
the contradictory clauses of the Act of 1832 — thus snatching
the vote away from men who had possessed it for anything up
to eight years.

Graham's proposals met with some resistance from Howick

(joint occupiers),[18] from Lord Campbell (chapel trustees),[19] and rather more idiosyncratically, from Lord John Russell, who seems to have stood almost alone in objecting that the clauses allowing claimants and objectors to appeal to the judges would trench upon the privilege of the House of Commons to decide disputed elections.[20] But the Bill passed without amendment, for the Peel Ministry enjoyed a secure majority in both Houses. Just how much advantage the Ministry derived from it subsequently, it is not easy to say. Contemporaries seem to have anticipated that many hundreds and possibly even thousands of successive and joint farm tenants would find their way onto the registers. But the overall numbers of tenants at will or occupiers in the counties of England had in fact peaked at 102,115 in 1842, and, being apparently already subject to attrition by other social and agricultural factors, had actually fallen to 100,026 four years later,[21] so that the gain cannot have been enormous. On the other flank, Campbell estimated that the Act of 1843 would disfranchise several hundred chapel trustees. A quick check shows that in West Sussex the three trustees of Ginger's Chapel, Billingshurst,[22] in East Surrey the four trustees of the Chapel in Reigate High Street,[23] and in North Warwickshire the eight chapel trustees surviving on the register in 1842,[24] were all struck off. The trustees had never been numerous, and now they were indeed almost wiped out, for only in the rarest instances, like that of William Chaney Worley, trustee in actual possession of a freehold chapel and land in Addlestone, West Surrey, was one able to survive into the new era.[25]

If, in framing the Registration Act of 1843, Peel's Ministry pursued any less easily avowed objective than that of administrative efficiency, it was presumably that of consolidating their support among the landed interest and the Anglican Church. Since the party disintegrated over the Maynooth grant in 1845 and the repeal of the Corn Laws a year later, they can hardly be said to have succeeded. Much worse, however, from Peel's point of view, than his failure to please friends was the fact that, for the sake of numerically insignificant electoral advantages, he antagonised enemies. The Act of 1843 made it look as though the government itself endorsed the popular view that the Tory party ruled the United Kingdom through the tenants at will, and the lesson was not lost upon the leaders of the Anti-Corn

Law League. Further, the assault upon the chapel trustees, launched simultaneously with Graham's inept Factory Bill of 1843, whose educational clauses would have required Dissenters to send their children to Church schools, made it appear that the Ministry was pursuing a policy of systematic aggression upon behalf of an increasingly Tractarian Established Church. The new image Peel had laboured since 1834 to give the Tory party vanished almost overnight. Wesleyan Methodists joined forces with Dissent, Dissent was confirmed in its already intimate relations with the Anti-Corn Law League, and the League, alarmed lest Peel succeed in fortifying the landed interest through the Registration Act, in turn began to consider how it might hit back at the government through the annual registration and the revision courts. In the 1830s the Conservatives had paid more attention to the registration than the Whigs had done. Peel and Graham's tactlessness now helped to bring into the field against the Tory party a combination of financial resources and ideological commitment which the Whigs never had possessed and never could have mobilised. Seldom can the careless pursuit of party advantage have rebounded quite so quickly and with quite such effect upon its authors.

Two major histories of the Anti-Corn Law League have been written, by Prentice (1853) and by Norman McCord (1958). Prentice treated the League's registration campaign as a thing of 1843–4, and made little reference to it for 1844–6, when it became effective. McCord paid more attention to the registration campaign, and referred to it in a chapter heading as 'The Great Fact'. But, in a chronologically ordered account, he too gave the impression that the campaign belonged to some middle period of the League's existence; and, in his final chapter, 'The Decisive Theatre', he returned to the situation in Parliament in 1845–6. The account which follows, in the remainder of this chapter, is intended, by contrast, to stress the decisive significance of the registration, the *'tremendous engine'*[2][6] with which the Anti-Corn Law League reached its climax in 1845–6 and achieved its object.

The League's tactics were evolved slowly, and the Registration Act of 1843 was passed at an important stage in their development. In the first of four phases, following the formation of the League in 1838, the leaders seem to have supposed that a small number of Reformers had only to state a

self-evident and divine truth and to repeat it often enough, as
the 'Saints' had done in their campaign against slavery, in order
to convert minds and overwhelm contrary interests. Accordingly all that was necessary was for Charles Villiers, the Member
for Wolverhampton, to bring in a motion for a committee of
inquiry into the operation of the Corn Laws, and the question
would make its own way among the existing Members of
Parliament. When Villiers's annual motions were annually rejected, the League's campaign entered a second phase, in which
the League leaders invited candidates for Parliament to pledge
themselves to free trade and began to run candidates of their
own wherever a pledge was not forthcoming. In January 1841
the League intervened in the by-election at Walsall, and later on
in the same year Cobden himself was returned, at the general
election, as the Member for Stockport. But Cobden then found
himself in a House of Commons markedly more hostile to free
trade than its predecessor: new initiatives were essential if the
League was to make any further progress, and in 1842 the Free
Traders' campaign passed into its third phase, when Cobden
wrote to George Wilson, Secretary of the League, asking him to
list the boroughs, divide them into categories, and attend to the
registration.[27]

In the mouth of a party agent this phrase 'attending to the
registration' would have meant persuading supporters to claim
the vote and objecting to opponents. There were certainly
constituencies where the League was engaged in these activities
by the beginning of 1843, and towards the end of the year *The
League* newspaper published Borough Electors Memoranda, in
order to remind its readers of the successive dates by which
they must possess or occupy a house, reside in the borough, and
pay their rates and taxes in order to qualify to register.[28] But in
1843 the main thrust of the League's attention to the register
appears to have been conceived in terms of the despatch of
propaganda to the existing electorate. In September the League
undertook to secure copies of every borough register, to bring
them to a central office in London, and to write weekly to
every one of the 300,000 electors who could produce a
majority in Parliament at the next general election.[29] 'The
problem', *The League* announced, 'is simply to find the
quantum of knowledge, and the means of conveying it, to the
electoral mind . . . .'[30]

1843 was a good year for the League. A feud among Tories allowed Bright to enter Parliament for Durham,[31] and in October the League's own concept of attending to the register appeared to have been crowned with success when the Free Traders captured the vacant seat for the City of London after every one of the 15,000 electors had been addressed five times through the press and the post.[32] Finally, a month later, the Free Traders won Kendal, one of the handful of new boroughs created in Schedule D of the Reform Act which had assumed a proprietorial aspect from the start, and where there had never previously been a candidate to challenge the interest of the House of Lonsdale.

Henceforth the League undertook to contest every borough, and at this point its luck ran out. The Free Traders were beaten at Salisbury, and in 1844 disaster followed humiliation. In four months the League was defeated at Devizes, Hastings and Exeter, and unable even to raise a contest and get to a poll in Huntingdon, Horsham and Woodstock. The League was rapidly being turned into a laughing stock, and still worse was to follow in July and August, when two Free Traders split the vote and allowed a Protectionist to come in at Birmingham. Further rebuffs followed at Cirencester and Dudley. Admitting that the League's propaganda was not making much impact upon the existing electorate, *The League* now professed to believe that the errors of electors *in esse* might yet be corrected by the recruitment of voters *in posse*,[33] and the League Council boasted loudly of the great gains they were making upon the registers of 112 out of the 160 towns which their agents had visited.[34] Their statistics may have helped to rally the failing hearts of the faithful, but the League leaders were nowhere near the point they had hoped to reach in November 1844, when, with a majority of Free Traders upon the borough registers, they would petition the Queen to dissolve Parliament and call a general election,[35] and the fact was that, whatever they might say in public, they were being forced to reappraise their tactics.

Hitherto the League leaders had taken it for granted that they must attend to the registration in the boroughs. This was understandable: everyone associated commerce and manufactures with the towns, and the recession of 1841–2, when tens of thousands of manufacturing operatives appeared to be out of work because they could not sell their goods overseas, and starving because they could not import corn from abroad, demonstrated the power of the colonels of agriculture to hold the captains of industry to ransom. But in 1844, when it became clear, as *The League* put it, that there were fifty (really 150?) boroughs 'hopelessly sealed against us', and that 'we cannot conquer by the boroughs alone',[36] new thinking was essential, and some unrecorded genius discovered the weak point in the enemy's armour. The League's approach to the registration of voters then entered its fourth and final phase.

The final stimulus almost certainly came with the League's defeat in its own backyard at the by-election for South Lancashire in May 1844. The Free Traders attributed their defeat to the 4000 tenant farmers alleged to have been enfranchised under the Chandos Clause in the Act of 1832 and the facility afforded for the registration of joint occupants in the Act of 1843.[37] Smarting under a defeat which was hailed by the Tory press as presaging the end of the League, they began to search for some means of reversing the verdict, and found it in the forty-shilling freeholder. At first sight this may appear strange. The 305,775 freeholders upon the registers of the English counties in 1842[38] appeared to be almost as favourably inclined towards the great landlords and as quick to resent the invasion of country districts by lecturers and agitators from the towns as the tenants at will themselves. The point the League leaders appear to have missed until 1844 was that in England there was no rigid distinction between the boundaries of boroughs and the boundaries of counties, and that, with the increasing tendency for the self-employed craftsmen and retail traders to live with their families in one quarter of a borough and carry on their businesses in another, there was a large and hitherto untapped body of urban freeholders many of whom already qualified as £10 householders in the boroughs in respect of their dwellings, who might be encouraged to lay claim to additional votes for the counties in respect of their places of work.

The discovery that 'every [non-resident] cobbler's stall, every [non-resident] butcher's shamble, every [non-resident livery master's] stable', could be made to yield a registered forty-shilling freeholder was undoubtedly made 'on the ground' in Lancashire, Cheshire, the West Riding and Middlesex, where the Free Traders had already been attending to the registration for several years, and not by the staff at the League's head-quarters.[39] Once Cobden's attention was drawn to it, however, he lost no time in making it his own. In a speech at Rochdale towards the end of November 1844 he said, 'Another light has dawned upon us within the last few months. We pledged ourselves some time ago to contest the boroughs ... but it never occurred to us that we could win counties in this country.'[40] The government of this country was 'at present in the hands of a class solely through the instrumentality of the Chandos clause'.[41] But there was another clause in the Reform Act 'which we of the middle classes ... never found out, namely, the 40s freehold clause. I will set that against the Chandos clause, and we will beat them in the counties with it.'[42] Middlesex was to be won in Hammersmith, Kensington and Chelsea,[43] Birmingham 'must put an extinguisher on the Gatton of North Warwickshire, and the Old Sarum of East Worcester-shire', and Wolverhampton and Walsall would liberate the Prime Minister's own division, South Staffordshire.[44] This was the new element Cobden now proposed to call into being to redress the balance of the constitution, and, in describing the new course in the League's campaign as a movement away from the boroughs to the counties, it will be as well to remember that it can more accurately be thought of as a movement away from the boroughs to the relationship between the boroughs and the counties.

In his history of the Anti-Corn Law League, Prentice, it is worth repeating, gave the impression that the registration movement was confined to the boroughs and to the years 1843–4. But anyone who will read *The League* newspaper will see that in November 1844 the campaign was switched to the counties, and that the League adopted both the propaganda and the tactics which were to carry it through to its final triumph. Peel, the message ran, was to be defeated with his own weapons: it was he who had 'detected the vulnerable point of the Reform Bill' and seen his way 'to the reconstruction of a great political party, even by means of the very measure which was the monument of its defeat ....'[45] In his great speech at the Merchant Tailors Hall in May 1837, he had exhorted his supporters to 'Register! Register! Register!', and so successfully had they followed his advice that 27 million people were now in thrall to 30,000 selfish landlords who had seized power through

the multiplication of their dependent tenants, and the registration of their votes.[46] Taking up Peel's own cry, and adapting
it to the season of the year, *The League* now urged its readers,
through its headlines, week by week before 31 January, to
'Qualify! Qualify! Qualify!', and subsequently, week by week
before 20 July, to 'Register! Register! Register!'

Right from the start it seems to have been determined that
the League would do more than merely employ agents to
discover men who already owned forty-shilling freeholds and
persuade them to make a claim to be put upon the register, and
that it would imitate the great landlords and actually manufacture votes. The League would invite men to invest their
savings in the purchase of votes, and in order to do this would
itself act through a Freehold Land Society as a political estate
agent or broker. In areas like Middlesex, Essex and Hampshire,
where the League's political objectives were consistent with and
became caught up in the movement of populations away from
the towns and the sale of plots for subsequent development and
owner occupation, there was a *bona fide* side to this. But there
was another side to the League's activities which seemed to
many of its contemporaries to cross the borderline between fair
and foul play. This was the decision to purchase houses (many
of which must have been £10 town houses), to divide their
ownership into shares, and to let them to tenants whose rents
would bring in to each of the many owners forty shillings per
annum in the form of a rent-charge secured against freehold
property. In this way a large house could be made to yield one
vote in the borough for the tenant and up to ten or more votes
in the county. This was a manoeuvre which would have been
banned under both the original Reform Bill of March 1831 and
the revised Bill of June 1831, both of which contained a clause
to the effect that no person was to vote at an election for a
knight of the shire 'in respect of any house by reason of the
occupation whereof he or any other person shall be entitled to
vote for any City or Borough'.[47] Following the acceptance by
the government of the Chandos Clause, which meant that both
the landlord and the occupant of a farm could vote in respect of
the same property, and quite possibly with a view to keeping
different kinds of property on the same footing, this had been
amended to read that no person was to vote for a county in
respect of any freehold house 'occupied by himself' which

would confer a vote for any city or borough.[48]

As for the rent-charge itself, that was not a new invention: long before the Reform Act almost every county could yield examples of votes being manufactured in this way, and in Buckinghamshire, for example, in 1805, the Marquis of Buckingham had purchased the redemption of the land tax upon the Hartwell estate of Dr John Lee, valued at £108 per annum, and had then divided it into fifty-one shares, which he gave away to his agents, dependants and friends, every one of whom was bound to vote as he was told.[49] The mass-production of rent-charges was universally condemned as an abuse, and the Whigs ought to have put a stop to the practice in 1832; but they had not, and Cobden did not hesitate to exploit the omission. It was easier for the small man to purchase a freehold, or part of a freehold, yielding a rent of forty shillings a year than it was for him 'to take a £10 house, furnish it, keep it, and live up to it'.[50] The League would encourage its supporters to invest their savings in this way, purchase suitable properties, advertise votes for sale, and pay the legal expenses. Thousands of working men excluded from the borough electorates would thus be enabled to make a take-over bid for the counties. Touching the exposed nerve of the Tory party, *The League* declared that the towns and the townspeople had an especial right to assert themselves in the county representation. South Staffordshire, it alleged, picking on Peel's home division, 'is theirs, for they have made it'.[51] The League leaders must have been delighted when they got the reaction they were hoping for; and the Tory *Birmingham Advertiser*, in response to Cobden's speech urging Coventry to take over North Warwickshire and Birmingham to seize East Worcestershire, denounced him for conspiring 'to overthrow the Reform Bill itself, and subvert the just division of electoral power which that Reform Bill established'.[52]

Cobden knew that he had found a winner. He laughed at the spectacle of the Tory press praising the Reform Bill, and accused the Monopolists of 'an infuriate quarrel with the very machinery by the dexterous use of which' they had turned that Act to the destruction of its framers.[53] The new strategy of carrying the war into the enemy's camp suited the psychological needs of a pressure group, and henceforth arithmetic, like moral fervour, was on the side of the Free Traders. It took, Cobden estimated, £5000 of capital to create a single £50 occupier, but an investment of £40—£50 would suffice to purchase a forty-shilling freehold.[54] Furthermore, the landlords had already, since 1832, created all the dependent votes they could.[55] The land was finite, their estates could not be stretched out like India rubber,[56] and they dare not imitate the League by dividing them into forty-shilling freeholds, though socially it would be very desirable if they were to do so. Commerce and manufactures, on the other hand, might be extended indefinitely (provided the Corn Laws were repealed), and, as if to prove the point, the League appealed for £50,000 one year, £100,000 the next, and £250,000 in the third. These were enormous sums by contemporary standards, and even then there was a multiplier effect to be taken into account, because the League's thousands would be spent in drawing out the savings of their supporters and in helping them to invest them.

It was a consequence of the League's change of strategy that, since there was no forty-shilling freehold franchise in Scotland, while that in Ireland had been abolished in 1829, the work could be accomplished only in the 158 seats for the fifty-two counties of England and Wales. Scotland and Ireland, therefore, fell back to the rear of the League's army, while the contest was carried on in the 119 county seats where *The League* thought that 155,000 new voters would neutralise the effects of the Chandos Clause.[57] No time was lost in starting the new campaign: on 7 December 1844 *The League* asked 'Which Counties the Free Traders should attack First?', and answered its own question with a list of thirty-four county constituencies, headed by South Lancashire, the West Riding, Middlesex, North Lancashire and North Cheshire. Week by week over Christmas and the New Year *The League* reminded readers thinking of purchasing freeholds that their transactions must be completed before the end of January if they were to qualify to make a claim to register in July. Time was short; something could be achieved straight away in the counties where the Free Traders' agents already had the matter in hand, but it must have been clear, even as early as December 1844, that the League would have to look beyond the qualification of voters in January 1845, their registration in July, and the appearance of the new lists on 1 December, to the next qualification of voters by 31 January 1846, the next registration in 1846, and the electoral roll which would be in force in 1847.

Right from the start, then, it was evident that the new campaign was to last fourteen months, and in the meantime the League leaders were in a quandary. The more thoroughly they impressed Peel with their ability to create thousands upon thousands of new votes in the English counties in 1846, the more likely Peel would be to forestall them by holding the next general election upon the registers of 1845. In order to counteract such a move, the moment the qualifying season was over, at the end of January, the League's agents were sent out into the counties to undertake the routine work of election agents, to examine the existing registers, and to make all the objections they could. The results were surprising and encouraging. In the boroughs where they had been working hitherto, there was an automatic annual purge of the register. In the counties, however, a man's name stayed on the register until it was objected to. The overseers might make objections, and it may well be that dead men did not remain upon the registers for long, and that they were not impersonated as often in the English counties as they were in Ireland. But the overseers lacked the inclination to be thorough, and the consequence was that the League's agents discovered much dead wood. In the counties, where contests which would have exposed the true state of affairs were rare, the dead wood had hitherto acted as a kind of Conservative con-trick. The moment the Free Traders began their investigations it became apparent that there were many places where their cause was not as hopeless as they had supposed. In addition to the prospect that they would be able to create new votes, there was the certainty that they would be able to extinguish many old ones. Although the League, referring, presumably, to South Lancashire, North Cheshire and the West Riding, boasted that its intervention left the registers fuller than they had been before,[58] there were many constituencies, like Middlesex, East Surrey and South Cheshire, where the immediate effect of the League's activities seems to have been to reduce the number of registered electors one year before adding to it the next.

Given its fanaticism and its anxiety about the register of 1845, it was almost inevitable that the League, in its turn, would resort to wholesale and systematic objections. When the summer came, and the registration season was in full swing,

23,000 forms of objection were made out in the League's office in Manchester, taken down to the constituencies to be signed, and returned to Manchester, where they were posted on 24 and 25 August, the last days allowed by law for the service of objections. 1800–2000 objections were made to Conservative voters in North Staffordshire, 1600–2000 to those in South Cheshire, 1370 to those in South Leicestershire, 800–1000 to those in North Warwickshire, and 934 to those in East Gloucestershire.[59] Viewed as a *coup de théâtre*, the League's intervention was a success, drawing attention to the Free Traders, and provoking cries of outrage from the Tory ranks. Viewed as a serious intervention in the electoral process, it appears to have been carelessly executed, and much of the evidence which was brought before the revision courts by the Conservative agents in the constituencies which had been attacked cast doubt upon both the capacity and the honesty of the League. In Cheshire the forms of objection had been signed when blank and returned to the League's office in Manchester, where the names of the persons objected to were filled in. In Warwickshire many of the objections signed William Worthington had in fact been forged by a Coventry weaver named Stafford. The League had not been meticulous, or even prudent in the choice of its agents, some of whom it was obliged to disown. Nevertheless, at the end of the day, the League, making no distinction between enemies struck off and friends placed on the register, claimed to have improved its relative standing by 2405 in the West Riding, 1831 in South Lancashire, 1492 in North Lancashire, 1520 in Middlesex, 942 in North Staffordshire, 936 in South Staffordshire, 899 in North Cheshire and 397 in South Cheshire, 754 in East Somerset, 553 in East Surrey, 328 in Buckinghamshire, 271 in East Gloucestershire, and 106 in North Warwickshire.[60]

No doubt ways could be found of contesting the accuracy of these figures, but the fact that the initiative had now passed to the League was driven home when it appeared that even before the registration of 1845 was complete the Free Traders were ready to start campaigning for the next one. On 15 November 1845 *The League* published a list of counties where Free Traders should be encouraged to buy forty-shilling freeholds before 31 January. The movement had now spread far beyond its original centres, in Lancashire, Cheshire, the West Riding and

Middlesex. In the north the campaign was being extended into Cumberland, Durham and Northumberland; in the Midlands, into Derbyshire, Leicestershire, Nottinghamshire, Rutland, Staffordshire, Warwickshire and Worcestershire; in the east, into Essex and Norfolk; and, further south, into Cornwall, Gloucestershire, Hampshire, Kent, Somerset, Surrey, Sussex and Wiltshire — in short, wherever there were towns or seaports with the populations to invade the shires. After a year's experience and preparation the League knew how to put ever more pressure upon Peel. How to win counties and how to win Peel were said to be perfect political synonyms,[61] and in December the League inserted advertisements in local newspapers everywhere between Brighton and Berwick, inviting Free Traders who were experiencing difficulty in finding freeholds to contact the agents of the League at their regional offices.[62] *The League* then gave a further turn to the screw by flagrantly advocating a policy of giving the register 'a lift'.[63] Residence was not a necessary qualification for the county franchise, and in places where there were not enough Free Traders to overwhelm the Monopolists *'One county and one division may help another.'* The men of Lancashire were invited to step over the border into Cheshire and acquire freeholds there,[64] and in due course the League claimed (or admitted) that, out of 726 persons newly qualified to make a claim at the next registration in Cheshire, 250 lived in Liverpool, 125 in Oldham, eighty-one in Ashton, and sixty each in Rochdale and Manchester.[65] Similarly, the inhabitants of London were being urged to acquire freeholds in Middlesex, East Surrey and West Kent,[66] and Cobden himself purchased an eighteenth part of a large house in Brighton in order to secure a vote in his native Sussex.[67]

With the failure of the potato and the spectre of famine in Ireland everything was now coming to a climax. In July 1845 there was a second by-election in South Lancashire and the Free Traders avenged their defeat the year before; early in 1846 there was a by-election in the West Riding, and the Free Traders achieved a triumph. These were two of the four constituencies (North Cheshire and Middlesex being the others) where the Free Traders had been attending to the registration for longest, and the moral, clearly, was that, given time, they were bound to succeed. Even more important, perhaps, was the fact that South Lancashire and the West Riding were large and influential

constituencies. Had not the single election of O'Connell for
County Clare in 1828 persuaded Peel and Wellington to emancipate the Catholics? Was it not popularly supposed that
Brougham's election for the West Riding in 1830 had made it
inevitable that there would be a Reform Bill? In a Parliamentary
system in which the constituencies were of such grossly dispro-
portionate sizes, Peel would be obliged to allow South Lancashire and the West Riding their full weight, or the League would
reopen the whole question of Parliamentary reform. *The League*
had already pointed out that the West Riding, with its two
Members, contained a larger population than Bedfordshire,
Berkshire, Buckinghamshire, Herefordshire, Hertfordshire,
Huntingdonshire, Monmouthshire, Oxfordshire, Rutland and
Westmorland (with their twenty-five MPs) put together,[68] and
other Free Trading newspapers had taken up the same theme.
The *Leicestershire Mercury* named twenty-four constituencies
with fewer than 300 electors each;[69] its contemporary the
Leicester Chronicle went one better a week later and named
174 constituencies with fewer than 1000 electors apiece;[70] and
the *Hertfordshire Mercury* printed an amusing little article on
the tiny seats Ministers sat for — not a man in the Cabinet
represented a borough of any size.[71] In point of fact the
League's relations with the Complete Suffrage Movement\never
became close, but Peel must always fear lest a mistake on his
part drive the League into more revolutionary courses, and start
a fire which, as the *Birmingham Advertiser* expressed it, would
engulf the landed interest, the aristocracy and the Church,
which were the institutions he really cared about.

The initiative in the annual registration had now passed from
the Conservatives to the Free Traders, and it was the League's
intervention in the counties as much as the failure of the potato
that had 'put Peel in his damn'd fright'. Graham's Registration
Act of 1843 had been expected to reduce the electioneering
aspect of the annual revisions by putting a curb on wholesale
and vexatious objections. But the League had now turned
electioneering into a year-long activity without a pause, had
exploited the provisions for objections to be sent through the
post, and had emerged virtually unscathed, because the revising
barristers took the view that, whenever an objection led even to
a minor alteration in the description of a voter, his place of
residence or the nature of his qualification, no costs should be

awarded.[72] Graham's Act was looking increasingly nugatory, and nothing, it now appeared, could save the electorate from the petty annoyances of party warfare whenever feelings were running high. One hope, however, still remained to the Tories who felt that the League's activities in giving the register a lift amounted to an unfair and 'foreign' interference in the constituencies,[73] and that was that the Appeal Court established by the Act of 1843 would hold that the purchase and division of properties by the League was illegal under the so-called 'Splitting Act' of 1696.

There were five judges in the Court of Common Pleas, and when Graham's Registration Act was passed in 1843 the Lord Chief Justice was Sir Nicholas Tindal, who had been appointed a judge in 1829. Associated with him were Sir Thomas Coltman (1837), Sir Thomas Erskine (1839), Sir William Maule (1839), and Sir Cresswell Cresswell (1842).

Tindal was born in 1776 and had pursued a political career as a Tory before being appointed a judge. He was MP for Wigtown Burghs in 1824 and for Harwich (a notorious Ministerial borough) in 1826, was appointed Solicitor General in 1826, and found himself a respectable seat at Cambridge University in 1827 before he became a judge in the Court of Common Pleas in 1829. He was distinguished for his 'grave urbanity, calm dignity, and invariable good temper',[74] and his 'tranquil inflexibility' was looked upon as the impersonation of British justice.[75] He had an interesting career, and among the cases with political connections which came before him were Norton's accusation against Lord Melbourne for 'criminal conversation' in 1836, the trial of the valet Courvoisier for the murder of Lord William Russell (Lord John Russell's uncle) in 1840, and the trial of MacNaghten for the assassination of Drummond, whom he had mistaken for Sir Robert Peel, in 1843. At the time Graham's Act was passed he was sixty-seven, and according to *The Times* looked older. He had a cold, dry personality, was the only judge on the English bench who could speak for an hour without making a grammatical mistake, professed none of the opinions which attracted the million, and had never been known to warm the hearts of a jury.[76]

Coltman, Erskine and Maule had all been appointed by the Whigs. Coltman had the misfortune to die of cholera in 1849 just as he was about to go the Norfolk circuit, and his obituary

notices were composed in haste and are unusually unin-
formative.[77] Erskine had presided over the spring assizes at
York in 1840, when the Chartist trials were held, and had been
praised for his conduct by the *Northern Star*. Unlike Coltman
and Erskine, Maule had sat as a Liberal Member of Parliament,
having been returned for Carlow borough in 1837 in gratitude
for the part he had played in the disputed Carlow county
election petition, when he must have come to know the Irish
registration system inside out. The fifth judge and the second
Tory, Cresswell, was also a political lawyer. He was returned for
Liverpool in 1837 and 1841, and was known as a strong Tory
who always supported Peel.[78]

As first constituted, therefore, the Court of Appeal in
registration cases contained three Whigs and two Tories. But
Tindal himself sat all the time, and, since it was the practice for
four out of the five judges to sit upon the bench each term, it
would be easy to make sure that Cresswell was on duty when
the registration cases were heard, so that the composition would
never be less than two and two. It is difficult not to suppose
that, as Graham watched his Registration Act setting up the
judges of the Court of Common Pleas as the supreme registration tribunal, he heaved a sigh of relief and said 'We shall be
safe with Tindal.'

In 1844 Erskine retired and was succeeded by Sir William
Erle. This was an interesting appointment. Erle had sat as
Liberal Member of Parliament for Oxford, and voted with his
party throughout the Irish registration battle. He never spoke,
and he did not seek re-election in 1841, but he was still
regarded as a Reformer when he was promoted to the Bench by
Peel and Lord Lyndhurst in November 1844. The appointment
was severely criticised in *The Times*,[79] and undoubtedly
widened the ever-growing rift between the Prime Minister and
his followers, but it is not even mentioned in the most recent
biography of Sir Robert Peel, and in these circumstances
it would be rash to speculate whether Peel's object was to win
over an opponent or to take politics out of the appointments to
the judiciary.

The first case to reach the Court of Appeal which it is
necessary to notice arose out of the registration of 1844, came
from Lichfield, and is known as Marshall *v*. Bown. Lichfield was
a constituency of a kind which, for the sake of simplicity, has

never yet been referred to in this book. Contemporaries regarded it as a borough, and it was included among the boroughs in the printed statistics laid before parliament, but it was in fact a 'county of a city', where the forty-shilling freeholders were entitled to vote. Bown was one of six persons claiming votes in respect of a house purchased by an agent named Gorton, let for £15 per annum and resold to Bown and his fellows, who thus received fifty shillings each per annum secured against freehold property. Marshall's objection was that the house had been purchased with the intention of creating votes, and the case came before Tindal, Maule, Cresswell and Erle (two Tories and two Whigs). Tindal's judgement, which was delivered in February 1845, was that, as the vendor had not been a party to the intention to create votes, the case did not come within the meaning of the Act of 1696.[80] The objection was held, therefore, never to have arisen. *The League* rejoiced in the decision, which, it claimed, had settled the issue, and added, with relief, that this was just as well, because Free Traders had already spent between £200,000 and £250,000 upon the purchase of votes in Lancashire, Cheshire and the West Riding alone.[81] *The League*'s figure, which would mean that between 4000 and 5000 persons had either registered their votes in 1844 or qualified by the following 31 January to register them in 1845, may have been an exaggeration, intended to impress both friends and enemies. But it is worth recalling that in these three northern counties the manufacture of votes had been put in hand long before the League leaders adopted the tactic and made it their own; and, since the electorate in South Lancashire increased from 18,666 in 1843 to 21,940 in 1844 and 24,179 in 1845,[82] while that in North Cheshire increased from 6380 in 1843 to 6888 in 1845,[83] and that in the West Riding increased from 33,863 in 1842 to 36,084 in 1845,[84] it is not impossible that *The League* was telling the truth.

The League was not, however, on equally sure ground in claiming that future purchasers would be certain to get their money's worth. Tindal had gone out of his way to stress that he was not giving judgement upon the merits of the objection, and had added that he and his colleagues would be willing to give an opinion upon this point if it were ever brought before them. It is not surprising that this was interpreted as an open invitation to the parties to pursue the matter at the next registration.

Accordingly, in the summer and autumn of 1845, the Monopolists made strenuous efforts to challenge claimants whose qualifications had been manufactured by the League, and, when their objections were overruled by the revising barristers – the barrister in Middlesex deciding in favour of votes created by the 'Equitable Joint Stock Investment Society', and the barristers in the West Riding upholding the claims of the new joint purchasers[85] – the matter moved swiftly towards the Appeal Court.

Appropriately enough, the perfect test case, known as Alexander *v.* Newman, arose at Lockwood, Huddersfield, in the West Riding, where the practice was most widespread. Joseph Bottomley was one of thirty-five persons who paid £1400 to Messrs Crosslands, mill-owners, in order to purchase land and cottages adjacent to their mill and occupied by their employees, and then leased the property back the same day to Messrs Crosslands for fifteen years at a rent of £70 per annum. Nobody disputed the facts, and even the motives were explicit and admitted. The agent employed to effect the transaction was an employee of the Anti-Corn Law League, who had inserted advertisements in the newspapers offering himself as the medium through which persons wishing to buy land for the purpose of securing votes could be put in touch with persons wishing to sell it with the object of creating them. The purchasers were not making an ordinary investment. They did not care about the nature and the situation of the property, which they had never seen, and had no object other than to acquire the right of voting. For their part, Messrs Crosslands had no liquidity problem: they had no need of the money from the sale, and their 'only object' was admitted to be the increase of 'the number of voters for Members to serve in Parliament'. In short, 'The said Messrs C and the thirty-five other persons entertain the same political opinions; and, though there was no immediate concert between them, the avowed and only object of the transactions on both sides was to multiply voices in the election of members of parliament . . . .'[86]

Nothing could have been clearer, and, when he heard that the four judges were to be Tindal, Coltman, Cresswell and Erle (once again two Tories and two Whigs), the Tory party agent still had some reason to hope that the Appeal Court would at last declare transactions engineered by the League illegal under

an Act which said that 'all conveyances in order to multiply
voices' at elections were void. In that case he was in for a shock.
The case was argued on 13 November 1845 and judgement was
delivered in January 1846. Tindal had the reputation of being
able to expound a statute in any direction he chose, and he
certainly lived up to it now. In his judgement he said that

> The statute names the conveyance only: it makes no refer-
> ence whatever to any contract for sale upon which a real
> conveyance was grounded, nor professes to deal in any
> manner with the estate or interest in the land which was
> affected by such contract of sale, nor provides for the
> revesting of the land which passed into the possession of the
> purchaser ... all which provisions might reasonably be
> expected, if a conveyance upon a real bona fide contract of
> sale, and not a fictitious conveyance only, was intended to be
> avoided on account of the motive upon which it was entered
> into.

In other words, the Splitting Act related only to a fictitious
conveyance where nothing changed hands or was intended to
change hands — a proceeding occasionally resorted to by noble-
men who wished to make dependent voters out of their retired
servants, and by landowners who wished to poll their game-
keepers.[87] But it did not apply to *bona fide* transactions, even
though these had as their avowed object the creation of votes.
The law abhorred covin, but in this case there had been no
secret reservation between the sellers and the purchasers; a deed
of conveyance had been prepared, the purchase money and legal
costs had been paid, and the property had without question
changed hands. The votes were therefore valid.

Tindal's judgement was given as 'the judgement of the court',
which meant that the four judges were unanimous. Even after
allowing for the fact that English judges were not like Irish
ones, and did not automatically divide along party lines upon
every issue, the fact remains that a career in politics was the
normal road to a judgeship, and that the judges handing down
this decision were divided politically, two and two. Why, then,
were they unanimous?

It is possible that the judges had but one concern, which was
to interpret the statute of 1696 correctly, and that they all

agreed, exactly, as lawyers, in their interpretation of the law. It is also possible that, while the strict letter of the statute should have applied to *bona fide* as to fictitious conveyances, the judges could see no way of enforcing a law which required them to distinguish between a sale which conferred a vote incidentally (as most sales of land did) and a sale made with the intention of creating a vote. Evidence that this is a plausible conjecture can be found in the minutes of the Select Committee of the House of Commons appointed to inquire into the activities of the League. Mr Henry Verrall denounced the agent who had purchased a house in Brighton and divided it up into eighteen rent-charges, and was going on to lament the prospect this opened up of the county being swamped by outsiders, when he was forced to admit under cross-examination that in the course of a career which had begun long before the League was ever thought of he had seen hundreds of ordinary commercial advertisements in which political influence was featured as one of the attractions of a property for sale.[88] The literal interpretation of the Act of 1696 would have voided innumerable transactions completed during the last century and a half, and the Select Committee of 1846 was asking for the impossible when it recommended that the provisions of the Splitting Act should henceforth be applied even to *bona fide* transactions if they were intended to create votes.[89]

But there is good reason to suppose that neither of these hypotheses contains the whole truth. When Tindal delivered the judgement of the court, he may either have been bound, as a lawyer, to say that the Act of 1696 did not apply to *bona fide* transactions, or he may have concluded that an ancient, frequently broken, and unenforceable statute should be set aside. But he was not bound to continue in these words:

> The object of increasing the number of freeholders at a county election is not an object, in itself, against law or morality, or sound policy. There is nothing injurious to the community in one man selling and another buying land for the direct purpose of giving or acquiring such qualification. The object to be effected is neither malum in se nor malum prohibitum. On the contrary, the increasing the number of persons enjoying the elective franchise has been held by many to be beneficial to the constitution, and certainly

appears to have been the leading object of the legislature in passing the late act for amending the representation of the people of England and Wales.[90]

Even in quiet times these would have been political sentiments. No dictate of legal duty required Tindal to deliver them, but he chose to express them, and, that being so, we must conclude that the judgement in the case of Alexander *v.* Newman was a political judgement. And, if it was a political judgement, then it was, in a sense, a 'Peelite' judgement, that the way to finish off the League was to give way to it, while simultaneously demonstrating to the Protectionists that there was no alternative: the judges would not enforce the existing law, and the Protectionists in Parliament would be unable even to attempt the much more difficult task of passing a new one.

Whatever the judges' reasons, the effect of their decision must ultimately have been devastating. For a time, it was true, an active Conservative agent, like the one in Hertfordshire, might be able to counter-attack manufactured claims because of 'the neglect and want of skill' with which they had been drafted.[91] Individual revising barristers, too, might discountenance claims which displeased them, as happened in Northumberland in 1846, when twenty-four persons, 'principally Scotchmen', claiming to register in respect of rent charges derived from houses at Alnwick, were struck off the list at one fell swoop by a revising barrister who exclaimed, with an air of triumphant self-satisfaction, 'There, now, *we have repelled the invasion of the Scots!*'[92] But we must not allow successful Tory rearguard actions of this kind to blind us to the fact that the judges' decision in the case of Alexander *v.* Newman gave the League the go-ahead to create as many votes as it could. Thousands of persons had already|purchased|property and found their way onto the registers in 1844 and 1845; thousands more were qualifying while the appeal was being heard; and thousands more still, we can safely assume, were hanging back, waiting for the legality of the purchase of votes to be placed beyond all doubt before investing their savings in this manner. The judges' verdict came too late to make much difference to the numbers purchasing property before 31 January and qualifying to register in 1846. But there seems no reason to doubt that, had Peel not repealed the Corn Laws, the Free Traders would have flocked onto the registers in 1847. Cobden was boasting, but not idly, when he said that with the *'tremendous engine'* of the forty-shilling freeholder he could have unseated 100 Monopolists in three years.[9][3]

Judgement in the case of Alexander *v.* Newman was delivered on 29 January 1846. Two days earlier Peel had introduced the Bill to repeal the Corn Laws, and five months later, when the Bill passed, he ostentatiously and dramatically heaped all the praise upon Cobden. The League leader himself continued for the remainder of his life to believe that the creation of the forty-shilling freeholders had frightened the landowning classes into submission. Whether Peel knew in advance, in January, exactly what course the deliberations of the Court of Appeal were taking, it is impossible to say, but he can scarcely have been in ignorance which way the wind was blowing. To the question 'Who repealed the Corn Laws?' two answers have hitherto been given: 'Richard Cobden' and 'Sir Robert Peel'. It is time to enter the name of a third candidate, Sir Nicholas Tindal, a man in his seventieth year, who died at Folkestone on 6 July, just ten days after the Bill had passed and Peel resigned. Reading between the lines of the many obituaries which drew attention to the fact that opinions about him varied,[9][4] it is possible to detect a sense of disappointment among the Tories that Tindal had somehow let the side down. Deserted by the judges, what were the poor Protectionists to do?

The tremendous engine was not, of course, the only influence at work bringing Peel to the decision to repeal the Corn Laws. There was the growing intellectual conviction that the arguments in favour of free trade were stronger than those against it, there was the immediate spur of the potato famine, and there was the Prime Minister's fear of the manner in which the League's propagandists might exploit a situation in which men were starving and bread was taxed. But politicians are not noticeably prone to change their minds as a result of the debates in Parliament, repeal was not likely to benefit the Irish who were going to starve, and, far from showing a disposition to convulse the country, the League was making a virtue of constitutionality. Scratch a Leaguer and you would find a special constable — why not, then, call the League's bluff? None of the traditional explanations for Peel's behaviour is sufficient in itself, and even when taken together they still leave something missing. That something can, however, be supplied when we realise that more than one crisis was coming to a head in the autumn and winter of 1845—6. In addition to the prospect of famine in Ireland, there was a crisis developing in the constituencies in England. The League had discovered how to register townsmen in the counties, and was reaching a position from which it could launch an effective assault upon the power base of the landowners and the Conservative party. Certainly many different causes were at work in 1845—6, and it is cumulative causes with which we have to deal. But the causes look much more cumulative when we consider how the story told in these pages helps to account not just for Peel's decision, but also for the comparatively ready acquiescence of the House of Lords. The peers in their territories would be the first to suffer if the League's registration campaign gathered momentum; rational peers had no cause to resist, and irrational peers, whose instincts were to die in the last ditch, were handicapped both by the fact that the judges had already spoken, and by the deeply rooted convention which placed the judges beyond the reach of criticism.

From the day the League was founded to the day it was dissolved, its leaders claimed to be acting outside party.[9 5] Certainly between 1839 and 1841 the Free Traders kept aloof from the Whigs, injured them by their intervention in the by-election at Walsall, and derided the Whigs' proposals for a small fixed duty upon corn. In 1845 *The League* alleged that after the general election of 1841 the Whigs had abandoned the registration in many divisions, including South Lancashire, East Gloucestershire and South Hampshire, and that its own agents had moved into a vacuum.[9 6] Even if that were true, it was not the whole story. In many constituencies the sense of identity between the Reformers and the Free Traders was much stronger than the distinction between the Whigs and the League. Even in 1841, when the Whigs were still in office, the Whig candidate at Walsall retired from the contest in favour of the candidate sponsored by the League, in order not to split the Liberal vote.[9 7] As the League's power increased, active Reformers rejoiced to see Peel's Ministry discomfited, and many of those who had given but lukewarm support to the Melbourne Ministry made common cause with the Free Traders.

The *Durham Advertiser* may have been a trifle indiscriminate in identifying the Whigs with the Liberals, the Radicals, the Leaguers, the Chartists and the Socialists,[98] but, from 1843 at least, newspapers of all political persuasions increasingly used the words Reformer, Liberal and Free Trader interchangeably. Thus the *Manchester Guardian* spoke of the man who had been selected 'by the friends of Free Trade as the candidate of the Liberal interest in South Lancashire'.[99] It is true that there were constituencies like Hertfordshire, where the Liberal press gave a rather guarded welcome to the arrival of the League agent;[100] Middlesex, where the local Whigs were accused of holding themselves aloof from the Free Traders;[101] and East Surrey, where two well-organised, active and distinct registration societies represented the Reformers and the League.[102] But they were almost certainly outnumbered by the number of constituencies where a single agent represented both the Reformers and the League, and in many places the League simply took over or bought out the Liberal machinery. In Liverpool the League and the Reformers coalesced, and in South Cheshire the Liberal agent, Mr Parry, represented the Anti-Corn Law League supporters.[103] In South Leicestershire Lawrence Staines, who signed the League's objections in 1845, had been 'for years past employed as an active agent, looking up new claims and objections on behalf of the Reform Society', and the Conservative agent was unable to distinguish between the authors of the wholesale objections made to Conservative voters in 1835 and those who were making objections ten years later.[104] In the West Riding Mr Flint, who was promoting the sale of forty-shilling freeholds for the League, was one of the secretaries of the registration association on the Liberal side,[105] and in Middlesex, where the exertions of the Anti-Corn Law League were said to have superseded those of the regular party connected with the county,[106] Mr W. H. James, who had acted for the Reform Registration Club for seven or eight years, admitted having changed masters because the League paid.[107]

It is clear that by 1845 the League and the Liberal party had drawn close together in the constituencies. The League required experienced agents, and the agents themselves and the Reformers generally were attracted by the League's aggressiveness and its apparently inexhaustible resources. In these circumstances the Whig leaders had no alternative but to embrace the League's cause if they wished to retain control of their own party, and Lord John Russell's Edinburgh Letter, in which he admitted that it was no longer worthwhile contending for a fixed duty, has to be seen in this light. Some of Russell's right-wing colleagues might complain, and hanker after an alliance with the Protectionists, but the fact was that at constituency level friend and foe alike identified the Free Traders with the Reformers. That being so, it was the Reformers who were the principal residuary beneficiaries when the Corn Laws were repealed in June 1846 and Cobden disbanded the League. The Free Traders are said to have taken an independent part in the revision courts in Birmingham in 1846,[108] but a majority of the League's employees accepted the termination of the campaign and were reabsorbed into the Liberal ranks. A glance at the local newspapers shows that in East Gloucestershire, South Hampshire and Hertfordshire the League's agent of 1845 had become the Liberal agent of 1846,[109] and, as Ostrogorsky noticed in 1902, T. N. Roberts, who had supervised the League's registration campaign, later became the chief agent of the Liberal party.[110] For this reason, it will not be inappropriate, in order to make a final assessment of the impact made by the Free Traders, to see how the Reformers fared at the general election of 1847.

In considering the results of the election it is essential to remember that the League's campaign to create forty-shilling freeholders had got into full swing in time for the 1845 registration only in Lancashire, Cheshire, the West Riding and Middlesex. In the other constituencies named by the League it was intended that the campaign should be intensified in 1846 and 1847. But, as *The Times* said with reference to the League's registration campaign and to Peel's surrender, 'The forces which were thus slowly but surely accumulating were spared the struggle to which they looked forward, and were led to the desired victory by the chieftain they were enlisted to fight against.'[111] The Corn Laws were repealed in June 1846, over a month before a man who had qualified in January need give notice of his intention to make a claim to be placed on the register, and presumably some, at least, of those whose purchases had been made with the sole object of bringing about the repeal of the taxes on bread never claimed the votes for which they had qualified. By the time the general election took place a further year had elapsed since the League had been dissolved, and all the League's propaganda and all the League's promotional activity had come to an end. In the meantime the Tory party had broken up, the urgency had gone out of politics, and there were fewer seats contested than at any general election since 1832.

This is the context in which we have to consider the seventeen clear gains, as compared with the general election of 1841, which the Reformers made in the English counties in 1847, and the one county seat where they replaced a Liberal-Conservative with a Reformer. Pride of place must be given to their successes in South Lancashire, where they had lost both seats in 1835, been beaten at a by-election in 1844, recovered one seat at a by-election in 1845, and now held one seat and won the other; to North Lancashire, where they had lost one seat in 1837, and now won one and saw the other retained by a Liberal-Conservative; to North Cheshire, where they substituted a Reformer for one of the two Liberal-Conservatives returned in 1841; to the West Riding, where they had lost both seats in 1841, recovered one seat at a by-election in 1846, and now held one seat and won the other; and to Middlesex, where they had held one seat in 1841, and now regained the other, which had been lost in 1837. That is to say that in the five constituencies where the registration campaign originated, and where it got under way before it became official League policy, the Free Traders made a clean sweep, the Reformers winning eight seats and the Liberal-Conservatives or Peelites two.

The Reformers enjoyed one other spectacular success, in East Surrey, where they recovered the two seats lost in 1835 and 1837, and little more was heard of the Conservatives until 1867. Elsewhere, round London, they won one seat in South Essex, lost in 1835, one in West Kent, lost in 1841, one in Hertfordshire, lost in 1841, and one in Buckinghamshire, lost in 1835; and it seems safe to say, as *The League* put it, that 'had the existence of monopoly been protracted to a new Parliament, we have little doubt that the League system of registration would have been found as effective in other counties as it proved to be in the West Riding of Yorkshire'.[112] Further afield, the pattern of Liberal gains in East and West Cornwall, West Norfolk and North Northumberland continued to follow the activities of the

League; but that did not mean that everywhere the League was active the Reformers made gains. The Free Traders had been busy in Southampton, but the Reformers could not improve upon the Liberal-Conservative who had been returned for South Hampshire at a by-election in 1842, and derived no advantage from the intervention of the League, unless the Liberal gain in the Isle of Wight is to be attributed to the votes of townsmen from the mainland, which seems unlikely. Bristol and Cheltenham did not capture East Somerset and East Gloucestershire as the Free Traders had hoped, and in West Somerset and West Gloucestershire the Protectionists actually made gains at the expense of the Reformers. Much the most skilfully conducted and stubborn resistance to the allied armies of Free Trade appears, however, to have been that encountered in the Midlands, where, for all their strenuous efforts and high hopes, the Reformers were unable to win a seat either in South Staffordshire and North Warwickshire (where Peel voted for the Reform candidate), or in South Leicestershire, where there was a long tradition of organised resistance by the county to town radicalism. It is a striking fact that the Conservative agents for South Cheshire, East Gloucestershire, South Leicestershire, North Staffordshire, East Sussex and North Warwickshire, who were chosen to complain of the activities of the League to the Select Committee of 1846, were all able to save their constituencies.

All in all, then, the swing was not enormous, and in many of the counties where a seat changed hands it was as a result of a delicate adjustment of local forces rather than as a consequence of a convulsion. In the counties a contested election was an expensive matter, and the parties were accustomed to use the annual revisions to keep their fingers on the pulse and extend or contract their claims accordingly. Thus in Hertfordshire and East Worcestershire, for example, after the two sides had counted up their gains and losses on the registers, the Conservatives were prepared to yield one seat without a contest and the Reformers were not prepared to start a fight in order to secure more than one.[113] In this realistic but rather cosy atmosphere it is not surprising that the candidates chosen by the Reformers were often reassuring ones. 'A Liberal candidate for a county, usually was not so spicy an article as one for a borough',[114] and in West Kent, for example, the Reformer was a practical farmer and was alleged to be a Protectionist.[115] In the Isle of Wight and in East Worcestershire the Reformer was a landlord and a farmer, and in Hertfordshire he was a landed proprietor with a pack of hounds.[116] Thus in county after county tactical adjustments were made, and the representation took on a little of the colour of the times. Changes took place in a gentlemanly way in the counties, but this should not blind us to the fact that somebody had first to behave like a cad and set the established order by the ears before changes could take place at all. The League had done just that, and not even the sophisticated protective devices employed by county society to reduce tensions and conceal from the general public the full significance of what was happening could hide the fact that the judges had not seen fit to challenge the League within the framework of the existing law, and that nobody had dared to change the law. The unsuccessful Tory candidate in South Essex hit the nail on the head when he attributed his defeat to the organised intervention of alien townees into the friendly countryside,[117] and he, at least, would have made no doubt that, one year after the struggle to repeal the Corn Laws was over, the actions of the League left a definite and measurable mark upon the general election of 1847.

6 Had the Corn Laws Not Been Repealed So Soon

Consistently with the stand they had taken while they were in opposition, Peel and his Ministers appear to have resolved, in 1844, to remodel the Irish registration system as closely as possible upon the English one. The revision was to take place every year, the solvent tenant test was to be re-enacted in its English form of 'clear yearly value', and both disappointed claimants and disappointed objectors were to be allowed to lodge appeals with the judges of the Court of Exchequer sitting in Dublin.[1] Thus far there were no surprises, and the draft Bill was not a conciliatory one. But Peel was tiring of party, and in an attempt to lay it to rest he conceded that existing electors should be allowed to remain on the registers until their certificates expired.[2] Most important of all, the government recognised that strict enforcement of the clear-yearly-value test would disfranchise anything up to two-thirds of the present electorate, and accepted the necessity to change the franchises.[3] Accordingly the Ministry proposed to lower the qualification for a freeholder from £10 to £5.[4] This clause in the Bill was welcomed by the Whigs and the Irish, but it was accompanied by another and counterbalancing one which would have conferred the franchise upon occupants rated at £30.[5] Not surprisingly, this innovation was denounced by the opposition as an attempt to introduce the Chandos Clause to Ireland and to create a dependent constituency, and proved fatal to the whole scheme.[6] The government had not introduced the Bill until April; the Irish Members, whom Peel had wished to please, preferred to go on as they were and to take their chance with a future Whig administration;[7] and in July Peel, with a carelessness that threw more than a little doubt upon his Ministry's sense of purpose, allowed the Bill to drop.[8]

By the time the Whigs came back into office the famine had begun to reduce the population of Ireland and to make inroads upon the electorate. There can have been few registered electors among the 2 million Irish who starved or emigrated, but the reduced demand for land changed the whole concept of what a responsible and solvent tenant could afford to pay. When the time came round, in November 1848, for the electors who had received new eight-year certificates in November 1840 to make fresh claims, many were unable to do so, and the number of registered electors fell: in the counties from 70,884 in 1847 to 34,107 in January 1849, and in the boroughs from 55,337 to 38,109, over the same period. Thus in two years the electorate fell from 126,321 in 1847 to 72,216 in 1849.[9]

In these circumstances a new Irish Reform Bill became a necessary part of the Whigs' measures of reconstruction for Ireland, and even the Tories agreed that something must now be done to build the Irish electorate up again. The Tories no longer stood to gain by procrastination, as they had done in 1840, and felt their interest lay in influencing legislation rather than blocking it. The broad outlines of the new Bill of 1850,[10] therefore, combined principles proclaimed by both Lord John Russell and by Lord Stanley in 1840. The registration system was to be reformed in the context of a modification in the Irish franchise, and the new registration procedures were to follow English ones as closely as possible.

The damaging dispute as to the interpretation of the terms of a beneficial interest and the amount that a responsible and solvent tenant could afford to pay was to be brought to an end by attaching the qualification, in both counties and boroughs, to the rateable valuations arrived at under the Poor Law Acts of 1838 and 1847. Nothing was said about leases, and the government proposed an uniform £8 rating occupation franchise in both town and country. In 1840 this would have been, it was argued above, a recipe for civil war. But circumstances had changed: O'Connell was dead, Ireland was prostrate, a rebellion had failed, its leaders had been convicted and transported to the penal settlements, Young Ireland was little more than a name, and for the first time since the Act of Union there was no immediate prospect of a land war. As for the registration, certificates were to be abolished, the registers were to be revised every year, and the dates set for each stage of the process corresponded to those prescribed in England. The Poor Law was now an effective part of the machinery of the Irish government, the clerks to the unions were to carry out the function of the overseers in England and draw up the draft registers, and the Whigs proposed that the clerks should put names on the registers 'automatically', as the overseers did in the English boroughs. Finally, the Bill proposed to take appeals away from the judges on assize, and send all appeals to the Court of Exchequer sitting at Dublin. At this time the four barons of the Exchequer were equally divided, two Tory and two Whig. On the Tory side, Pennefather, who had been an out and out 'responsible and solvent tenant' man, had been joined in 1841 by Lefroy, appointed by Peel; ranged against them were Richards, one of the two 'beneficial interest' judges who had defied the opinion of a majority of his colleagues, and Pigot, who had been Solicitor General and Attorney General for Ireland in Melbourne's government, and was appointed by Russell to succeed Brady in 1846.

The balance among the judges may have contributed to the feeling among all parties that this time the Bill must pass, and in the House of Lords Stanley did not attempt to wreck the Bill, as he would have done ten years earlier. Instead, the Earl of Desart moved one amendment, to raise the franchise in the counties to £15, and Stanley himself moved a second, to ensure that every man must first make a claim to have his name placed upon the register—which would have made the Irish system resemble the English one for counties, rather than that for boroughs (the stronger part of the English arrangements).[11] When the Bill returned to the Commons, the Ministry compromised upon a figure of £12 for the county franchise, and rejected the amendment requiring every voter to make a claim to have his name placed upon the register.[12] The new Irish Reform Act thus passed through the two Houses without the obstruction which had brought disgrace upon the Conservative opposition, and indeed upon Parliament, in the 1830s. Lord John Russell had secured a new Reform Bill for Ireland in the guise of a registration Act, and had linked the franchise to an ascertainable qualification in the assessment to poor rates; Stanley had secured the abolition of the certificates, an annual revision, appeals both ways (by objectors as well as claimants), and franchises high enough to safeguard the Tory strongholds in the Irish boroughs and to prevent the Reformers from making a clean sweep in the counties. In this last respect it could be argued that the Whigs conceded too much, and the first register compiled under the new Act revealed a further fall in the borough electorate, to 28,301. In the counties, on the other hand, the number of registered electors leapt to 135,245, and in Ireland as a whole the electorate increased to 163,546 in 1850, 179,488 in 1852, and 196,703 in 1860.[13] It was enough to provide for what passed by the standards of the time as a viable political life: a higher percentage of the voters now possessed *bona fide* qualifications, statistics could at last be handled with some confidence, and politically, at least, Ireland was better off under the Act of 1850 than it ever had been before.

Lord Chief Justice Tindal had declared the splitting of property in order to create votes to be legal, and following the repeal of the Corn Laws and the dissolution of the League in 1846 it must have appeared unlikely that the genie which he and Cobden had let out of the bottle could ever be put back in again. Contemporaries looked forward with apprehension to the former League leaders continuing to attempt to bring pressure to bear upon the aristocracy and the government of the day through the creation and registration of voters in the counties, and to the likelihood that others would follow in their footsteps, imitate their tactics – and, possibly, their success. But in 1846 Cobden and Bright had no agreed objective for the future: the new movement for the creation of county voters through the operation of Freehold Land Societies originated in Birmingham, and it is worth stressing that, right from the start, it did not aim to create rent-charges and votes through the large-scale purchase and division of house property. Although this was one of the practices which Tindal had declared legal, and there were perfectly good reasons in ordinary life for the creation of some rent-charges, just as there were for the creation of some tenants at will, there seems to have been a feeling that the mass-production of rent-charges was reprehensible. While it was understandable that the League should have resorted to it in the heat of the moment, any attempt to perpetuate and to extend the practice in calmer times would be contrary to the spirit of the constitution, and quite possibly self-defeating.

The Freehold Land Society movement was the brainchild of James Taylor (1814—87), a member of a tightly knit Baptist family of hard-working and self-taught Birmingham artisans. On new year's day 1841 Taylor took the pledge; with the wages he then earned he and his family were able to move year by year, from one house to another, each one more expensive than the last, until, by the end of Peel's Ministry, he was living at Temperance Cottage, which he had erected himself, possibly through the medium of a Building Society. He had not been a member of the Anti-Corn Law League, and he attributed the beginning of the Freehold Land Society movement to his experience at the general election of 1847, when he went to cast his vote and saw 'hundreds of hard-working men, standing and looking on, grinning and yawning over the poles which separated them from the voters'.[14] Taylor thought they ought to have votes, and in order to supply them he determined to follow up the more legitimate side of the League's tactics by creating genuine forty-shilling freeholds in the form of allotments.

Taylor's motives were political: the margins of his prospectus advertised County Votes for Working Men and Freeholds for the People, and in a manner reminiscent of the League he exhorted his subscribers to qualify and register. His scheme, which was countenanced and encouraged by Scholefield and Muntz, the Liberal Members for Birmingham, soon came to bear all the marks of a classic attempt by the big-town Radicals to invade the surrounding countryside. When the Protectionist agent for North Warwickshire objected to Taylor's freeholders at the annual revision courts, Taylor himself was drawn into undertaking the work of a constituency agent, and in due course he chose to make a point by informing the members of a Royal Commission that the officers of the Birmingham Freehold Land Societies were elected by 'annual Parliaments, vote by ballot, and universal suffrage'[15] (i.e. that all the members, men, women and children, participated in the elections every year). Yet, when all this has been said, it is clear that Taylor's motives were less exclusively political than those of the League. Cobden had said a lot about the industrious classes securing the franchise, and, in order to create votes and put pressure upon

Peel, had been willing to trade upon the working man's desire to own a plot of land. But Cobden, we may suspect, had not really cared who possessed the votes so long as the votes were cast in the right way, and a majority of those who purchased votes through the offices of the League were, it seems safe to assume, well-to-do. Taylor, on the other hand, truly did aim to satisfy the desire of the urban artisan to have a property of his own, and his objectives were social and philanthropic as well as political.

Taylor's first thought appears to have been to model the Freehold Land Societies exactly upon the Building Societies, and to encourage working men to club together in a society which would purchase plots as the united subscriptions of its members enabled it to do so, allocate them by ballot, and continue to collect both rents and subscriptions from all its members until all their needs were satisfied and the ownership of the plots passed from the society to its members. It was indeed essential if the members of a Freehold Land Society were to have confidence in each other and in the society, and if they were ultimately to be secure in their titles, that the rules of a Freehold Land Society and its position in law should resemble those enjoyed by a Building Society under the Act of 1836 (6 and 7 William IV c.32). But Taylor could not simply organise a Freehold Land Society and register it as a Building Society, because it was not clear that the Act of 1836 allowed Building Societies to own land.[16]

There was one obvious way round the difficulty. This was to persuade affluent and committed Reformers, operating in advance of the means of the societies, to invest in working men; to purchase estates themselves and hold them in trust for the societies, lay them out and divide them into plots, and make the plots available to individual members as the united subscriptions enabled the societies to advance the purchase money. Some of the early societies appear to have operated in this way, but the supply of rich political philanthropists was limited, and Taylor's own solution to the problem, which opened the way for the Freehold Land Society movement, offered the societies much better security. Taylor advised the officers of each society to select the estate they wished to buy, and to purchase it through trustees. The trustees should then mortgage the entire estate to the society and execute a deed undertaking to hold the land for the purposes of the society, to divide it into lots, and to sell the individual allotments to the members. As each member took up his allotment, a three-cornered transaction would then take place. The trustees would repay the appropriate part of their mortgage to the society, the society would advance the purchase money to the individual member, and he, in turn, would buy his allotment from the trustees, mortgage it to the society, and repay the society over a period together with interest. The societies themselves would thus never own land, while the members could then use their plots for gardens or build on them (with the aid of another advance and another mortgage from a Building Society). The difference between Taylor's societies and the so-called Freehold Land Society which had once operated on behalf of the League was that the League had been engaged in cash sales where Taylor was lending money against mortgages.

The new scheme received official blessing when Taylor raised with Tidd Pratt, the Registrar of Friendly Societies, the propriety of calling a Land Society a Building Society, and received the accommodating answer, 'it doesn't matter what it is: if you want the benefit of the act, you must declare it a building society whether it is one or not'.[17] For the purposes of the Act, then, Freehold Land Societies became Benefit Building Societies, and the rules of the Birmingham Freehold Land Society were certified on 27 December 1847 in the name of the Birmingham and Midland Counties Benefit Building Investment and Land Society.

Taylor's scheme secured for the members the advantages of bulk purchase, and this first society made an auspicious start. Land which the owner had refused to sell in small plots for less than 3s 4d a yard, was bought *en bloc* at a price which enabled the society to put its members in possession of their plots at a cost of 1s 1d per square yard.[18] The earliest subscribers to the new movement were thus able to purchase their plots, and their votes, for the astonishingly low sum of £19—£20 each, and loud boasts were then made that the political complexion of the Birmingham region of North Warwickshire was being transformed. The movement spread rapidly across the Midlands, and when Newdegate, who, as one of the two Protectionist Members for North Warwickshire, was one of the men most immediately threatened by the new development, raised the matter in

Parliament in June 1849, Bright claimed that the Freehold Land Societies now had 700 members in Wolverhampton, 700 in Derby, 450 in Coventry, 300 at Stourbridge, 150 at Dudley, and 100 at Stafford, and that the movement was spreading beyond the Midlands to Worcester (eighty members), Cheltenham (200), Sheffield (300), Bradford (140), Shields (200), and London, where there were 5000. Bright believed that, altogether, there had been called into existence a body of between 10,000 and 11,000 men who were thus working out their own political enfranchisement.[19]

Throughout 1848 Cobden and Bright were pursuing schemes of their own. Cobden was interested in national housekeeping and the reduction of the budget to the levels of 1835, and the promotion of peace among nations through free trade; Bright in the creation of a new political party based upon the League's former supporters in the North of England. Unable to make much impact either upon public expenditure or upon Palmerston's handling of foreign affairs, Cobden now began to regret that Peel had yielded so easily and that the Corn Laws had been repealed so soon. Had the landlords' resistance been prolonged, the League would now, by the manufacture of votes, 'have carried half the counties in England'.[20] Before the end of the year Cobden was ready to 'begin [again] where the League left off', and to go for the registers and the mass-production of forty-shilling qualifications;[21] and in January 1849 Cobden and Bright came together again, at Manchester, in a new combined Financial and Parliamentary Reform Movement. Convinced that 'the aristocracy are afraid of nothing but systematic organisation and step by step progress',[22] Cobden then joined forces with James Taylor in Birmingham and Sir Joshua Walmsley, MP for Leicester and the organising genius in London, and gave his name to the formation of a National Freehold Land Society with the objective of doubling the county electorate in seven years. Bright, too, spoke of 'working the constitution so as to reform it through itself',[23] and the movement spread like wildfire. In 1850 220 public meetings were held and 120,000 tracts distributed, and before the end of the year there were eighty societies, with 30,000 members. Two years later there were 130 societies, with 85,000 members, and by that time £790,000 had been paid into the movement, and 19,500 sites worth forty-shillings had been allocated.[24]

It all looked reminiscent of the heady days of the agitation for the repeal of the Corn Laws, but appearances were deceptive. There had always been an ambiguity about the movement, and a difference of outlook between the members of the societies, most of whom were motivated primarily by the desire to possess allotments or building sites of their own, and the politicians publicising the scheme, who aimed to create and mobilise votes in order 'to bring the Government into greater harmony with the wants and wishes of the majority of the people of this country'.[25] Viewed as a campaign for putting men in possession of small plots of land and reinforcing the base of the social pyramid, the movement was a success, and technical improvements in the legislation concerning Building Societies were to ensure that it continued to prosper far into the future. Viewed as a means of enlarging the county constituency, however, it was a failure. Year by year the addition to the registers was small, and not even in North Warwickshire, where the movement originated and Taylor himself conducted a League-style campaign of objections to Tory electors in 1851, were the Reformers able to unseat Newdegate and his fellow Member, Spooner, at the general election of 1852.

There were many reasons for this failure, and the first one was the attitude of the revising barristers and the Appeal Court. Tindal had established the legality of splitting property in order to create votes, but a serious question arose as to the exact moment at which a man who was in the process of purchasing a freehold by paying off a mortgage could come onto the register. Some of the more optimistic and naive promoters of Freehold Land Societies may even have supposed that, thanks to the Act of 1696 (7 and 8 William III c. 25), which laid it down that mortgages were not to be allowed to bar the proprietors of freeholds from voting, the new owners of these mortgaged allotments would be able to come onto the registers at once. However that may be, the revising barristers took the view that, although a mortgage was not in itself a bar to the franchise, a mortgaged estate, like any other, must be worth forty shillings a year to the owner, over and above all charges, if he was to qualify.

The first case to reach the Appeal Court was known as Copland *v.* Barnett,[26] and concerned George Brooks, who was a member of the Chelmsford and Essex Building and Investment

Society. Brooks's estate, which must have been a large one, was worth £8 per annum, but he had received an advance of £65 from the society to purchase it, and he was still paying fifteen shillings a month to the society. His annual charges amounted, therefore, to £9, and the revising barrister, who had concluded that he had no beneficial interest from the estate, struck his name off the register upon objection. When the case reached the Appeal Court, in November 1848, the four judges were Lord Chief Justice Wilde, who had been Whig Member for Worcester before Russell selected him to succeed Tindal in July 1846, Coltman and Maule (see above, pp. 89–90), and Williams, who had never been an MP but had been appointed by Russell in October 1846. All four judges, therefore, were Whigs, and they had no hesitation in confirming the decision of the revising barrister. Mortgages were as old as freeholds, similar questions had arisen time and again, and they rested their judgement upon precedents dating from the period between the Revolution of 1688 and the Reform Bill.

No attempt was made in the case of Copland *v.* Barnett to determine what proportions of the monthly payments of fifteen shillings represented interest and the repayment of principal. This omission led to loud complaints from the Freehold Land Societies, and three years later another case (Beamish *v.* the Overseers of Stoke) was taken to the Appeal Court.[27] Josiah Smith Beamish was a member of the Coventry and Warwickshire Benefit Building and Investment Society. His estate was worth £6 per annum, and his annual payments amounted to £11 14s, of which £8 18s went to repay the principal, £2 10s was for interest, and six shillings for the expenses of the society. The four judges were Lord Chief Justice Jervis, who had been Whig MP for Chester for many years before he succeeded Wilde in 1850, Maule, Williams, and Talfourd, who had been the Whig Member for Reading until he was appointed by Russell in July 1849. Once again, then, all four judges were Whigs, and, had they felt able to accept the distinction between the interest payments which were a charge upon the estate and the repayments of principal, and had they been prepared to take into account the proportion of the holding which was then clear of mortgage, they might have found grounds to reverse the revising barrister's decision and restore Beamish to the register. This they refused to do, and the small man who was purchasing an allotment through a Freehold Land Society was thus put at a disadvantage compared to an ordinary proprietor, who could mortgage his estate to any amount and still have only the interest on the mortgage counted against him as a charge.[28] It was not until 1863 (when Erle was Lord Chief Justice) that a more favourable decision was obtained, in the case of Robinson *v.* Dunkley.[29] By that time, however, the Freehold Land Society movement was no longer thought of as the spearhead of the Reform movement.

The attitudes of the revising barristers and the Court of Appeal meant that there could be no short cut for the working man through the Freehold Land Societies to the register of voters, and can be taken to account for the lack of impact which the movement made upon the counties in the general election of 1852. But that did not mean that the participants would not qualify eventually, when all their charges had been paid, and the Reformers still had some grounds to hope that significant political developments could eventually be engineered in this manner. But even here there were misconceptions, and many of the Reformers do not appear to have thought the consequences of the movement right through to the end. The plots lay just beyond the built-up area of the large cities and boroughs, and well within the radius of seven miles in which a man could qualify, and could be obliged to qualify, for a vote in a Parliamentary borough. When the mortgages to the Freehold Land Societies were paid off, there would be three categories of allotment owner. The first group would be those who already occupied £10 houses and qualified for votes in the boroughs: they would qualify for additional votes in the counties in respect of their allotments. The second group would consist of those who occupied houses worth less than £10 and did not yet qualify for votes in the boroughs: they would now, if the combined value of their two properties brought them up to the level of a £10 householder, be obliged to register their votes in the boroughs, where from the point of view of the political engineers they would be superfluous. The third group would consist of those who occupied houses of lesser value (or who did not in the sense of the Act occupy houses at all), the combined value of whose holdings would not qualify them for votes in the boroughs, and who would qualify to vote in the counties in respect of their freeholds. The whole situation was thus much more complicated than anyone had anticipated. To the philanthropist who wanted to add to the overall number of the self-respecting working class upon the registers, this scarcely mattered; but, to a political schemer who wanted to register votes in specific constituencies and to win counties, it posed serious problems. The most reliable group, from his point of view, would be the first, the men who were able to qualify twice, in respect of separate properties in the boroughs and in the counties. But, then, the further complication arose that these were the very men who were most likely to develop and build upon the plots they had bought on the edge of the town. When they did this they would give up rented accommodation in the inner town in order to go and live as owner occupiers upon the salubrious outskirts, and they would then, if their new houses were of £10 value, find themselves obliged once again to come off the lists of county voters and register their votes in the boroughs. The answer to the question 'Where did all the manufactured county freeholders go to in the 1850s and 1860s?' is that many of them eventually went back onto the borough registers, where some of them, at least, had already been when the Freehold Land Society movement began.

Cobden was, perhaps, the only man who possessed the organisational skills to make anything of a situation as complicated as this, and a further reason for the failure of the Freehold Land Society movement must lie in the attitude of Cobden himself. Cobden had no confidence in the political maturity of the masses. 'Immediately after the repeal of the Corn Law, he confessed that on the question of the suffrage he had gone back',[30] and year by year after 1846 the suspicion grew, among the real Reformers at least, that, although Cobden spoke of employing the forty-shilling freeholders and the Land Societies to pull down the monopoly of the landed aristocracy, he valued the forty-shilling freeholder scheme, with its requirements of steadiness and thrift, as a means of thwarting demands for universal suffrage.[31] Harking back to the campaign for the repeal of the Corn Laws, and regretting the lack of a definite objective in the present movement, Bright thought that, instead of just trying to qualify more urban artisans in the counties, as though that were an end in itself, it would have been 'more effectual to have started for Parliamentary Reform, and *for this* to have set in motion the forty shilling freeholds'.[32] But

Cobden was the prince of agitators, and, ruefully, Bright was compelled to recognise that a Reform movement led by the Freehold Land Societies could neither prosper without Cobden nor, given his present attitudes, with him. Bright might have added that there was a difference between the League's agitation in alliance with the Reformers for a specific object and against a Tory government, and this derivative campaign against Whig Ministries and for an indeterminate object.

Because Cobden himself was not prepared to engage all his gigantic energy in this one cause, and because Cobden and Bright did not see eye to eye, all the other problems connected with the Freehold Land Society movement appeared much more daunting than they would otherwise have done. First, it asked too much of the trustees who purchased the estates. Secondly, there was trouble within the societies themselves: those which did not distribute allotments by drawing lots did not prosper, and, in those which did, the Dissenters, whom Cobden had hoped to attract, objected on principle to the drawing of lots.[33] Thirdly, difficulties arose among the allotment holders: some, who prospered, wanted to extend their holdings and become substantial proprietors,[34] while others, who had a struggle to complete their purchases, were driven by their necessities into frequent sales.[35] Both reduced the number of voters reaching the registers. Fourthly, the sponsors suffered what was, perhaps, their greatest disappointment when they discovered that members who had completed their purchases and taken possession of their freeholds showed an alarming tendency to refuse to go to the poll, or even to change their politics and adopt the Conservative manners of the counties.[36] Finally, it soon became apparent that the mass-production of freeholds was a game at which two could play — as the Tory agents had pointed out when they complained of Peel's precipitate surrender in 1845—6. Newdegate himself, the Protectionist, and the first MP to be threatened by the formation of Taylor's Land Society, founded and fought back through a rival Land Society of his own;[37] and, writing in 1866, W. W. Barry said that the most extensive of the surviving societies was the Conservative Land Society, enrolled under the Act of 1836 as the Conservative Benefit Building Society.[38] Far from changing the balance of power in the counties, the whole movement was easily accommodated within the traditional structures: with a frown from the Whig judges the genie withered in the open air, and for the Reformers the moral was that the way ahead lay, not with this politically rather eccentric manifestation of the self-help ethic, but through a second Reform Bill.

The working classes were not, as such, excluded from the political system, and legally the same opportunities were available to the Chartists as to the League and the Freehold Land Societies. In the first place, it was open to them to make themselves a nuisance. Even with the existing franchises enough Chartists were, or could easily have been, registered, in every constituency, to make objections both to their opponents and to their employers. Men whose 'chains' rub do not usually pass up the opportunity of irritating those who have 'enslaved' them, even if they cannot hurt them.

In the second place, there were 'popular' constituencies, like Bath, Carmarthen, Coventry, Finsbury, Oldham and Tower Hamlets, where the electorate returned a middle-class Radical who supported the Charter, if not a working-class and Chartist MP. In some of these constituencies working-class electoral and registration committees formed the backbone of the local Radical party organisation, and there was ample opportunity for a would-be activist to serve a political apprenticeship and learn the tricks of his trade.

In the third place, there were marginal constituencies, which it would have been worth the Chartists' while to cultivate. Birmingham, Blackburn, Bolton, Carlisle, Greenock, Halifax, Ipswich, Leeds, Macclesfield, Norwich, Nottingham and Worcester were all boroughs where the Chartists either had or thought they had a chance, and where they might have improved their prospects by a tacit coalition with the Reformers, by steady, patient, sustained application to the qualification of voters throughout the year and for many years, and by a carefully prepared and surprise campaign of wholesale objections launched at the critical moment in the run-up to the register upon which the next election was likely to be fought.

Finally, although the large boroughs appeared to offer the more fruitful ground for Chartism, as they had done for Free Trade, there was no reason, in theory at any rate, why the Chartists should not also have invaded the counties. The League and the judges between them had opened the door to the creation of rent-charges and forty-shilling freeholds, and there was no reason why working men too should not combine together in clubs in order to help each other over the line. They already contributed to benefit clubs and burial clubs, to friendly societies and to trade unions, in order to insure themselves against the many hazards of sickness, unemployment and death. The Chartists among them subscribed in large numbers to O'Connor's land scheme, and men who were not crippled by jealousy of each other's good fortune, and were willing to draw lots for a smallholding, could, with other priorities and different tactics, have pooled their resources in order to purchase rent-charges upon freehold property.

The Chartists achieved one great triumph when they secured the return of O'Connor for Nottingham in 1847. For the rest, they succeeded in less than it appeared to be within their power to do. The reason is not far to seek, and lies in the ambivalence of their attitudes. Leaders and rank and file alike never could make up their minds whether they wished to work within the existing electoral system, to make compromising pacts with other parties, engage in the rough and tumble of the registration, and accomplish practical results, or to stand aloof and keep their hands clean. Chartism peaked three times, in 1838–9, 1842 and 1848, and each time the climax came in a depression of trade not long after a general election – when it ought, to have been effective in the registration, to have come eighteen to twelve months before one. In 1841 the leaders fell out over the policy of an electoral alliance: O'Connor advised working men to vote Tory, while Gammage and many other Chartist leaders refused even to contemplate an alliance with either Tories or Whigs, or, as they put it, to link 'truth and error, virtue and vice'.[39] In the mid-1840s the Chartists did set up national and regional electioneering committees, and are said to have made some attempt to 'place' the leaders and 'to concentrate money and energy in those areas where radical candidates stood the best chance of success'.[40] But in 1847 as in 1841 we hear of constituencies where, before deciding whether to contest the seat, the Chartists waited until a general election had been called. In 1847, too, O'Connor himself played down the political possibilities of his land scheme, angled it towards the withdrawal of surplus labour from the market and a return to the soil, required his allottees to pay rent, and missed a great opportunity to create a body of independent electors in the English counties.[41] Two years later, when his own scheme was wound up, and he lent his support to the agitation to create county voters through the medium of the Freehold Land Societies, he was denounced by both Harney and Jones for his willingness to 'garrison property'.

It is clear that the Chartist movement as a whole never advanced far beyond its original and favourite tactic, which was to exploit the contrast between the show of hands and the poll. It cost nothing to bring the masses to the show of hands, to nominate a Chartist candidate, to 'elect' him by a tremendous majority, to withdraw him before the poll, and to draw attention, after the formal declaration, to the difference between the two results. Thus, in 1841, Bronterre O'Brien (who was in prison) was proposed at Newcastle, while Harney and Pitkeithly contested the West Riding, 'where they carried public opinion in favour of the Charter'. The same technique was still being employed in 1847, when Harney challenged Palmerston at Tiverton, and other Chartist candidates contested the show of hands at Blackburn, Greenwich, South Shields and Stockport.[42]

Before we conclude that the Chartists were impractical visionaries who always were in danger of subsiding into an unimpressive federation of non-electors clubs, it is worth noticing that there was one point about the electoral system which they appear to have understood much better than anyone else. This was that none of those involved in the operation of the registration machinery and the conduct of elections was chosen in the open. The Chartists appreciated that the Reform Act had provided a stimulus to the (already by no means negligible) activities of party agents, many of whom were land-agents or solicitors, who regarded the management of a constituency as an extension of their day by day, and confidential, activities on behalf of the propertied classes.[43] As for the officials, these were all appointed, away from the publicity of an election, by the prerogative and executive power of the state. Derek Fraser has shown how the overseers, who were chosen by the magistrates, who were in turn recommended by the Lord Lieutenant and appointed by the Crown on the advice of the Home Secretary, were able to turn their tenure of office to electoral advantage by allowing opponents to fall behind with the payment of rates and concealing the fact from the enemy agent.[44] There are enough indications in this book to suggest that the decisions of the revising barristers, who were appointed by the senior judge on each circuit, and the judges, who were appointed by the Crown at the instance of the Prime Minister and the Lord Chancellor, were not always devoid of political, and even party political, content. It was this, perhaps, more than anything else which led the Chartists to feel that nothing had changed in 1832, and convinced them that it made no difference to them who were in power, Whigs or Tories. Historians have concentrated upon the six points of the Charter. But by far the greater part of the Charter relates to the provision of new and more honest machinery for the registration of electors and the supervision of the poll. In future, the Chartists proposed, both the registration and the return should be carried out by a single official, who should be elected annually at the same time as the Member of Parliament.[45] Only when they had confidence in the machinery, would the Chartists be willing wholeheartedly to contest the elections; and it is scarcely to be wondered at that, until that day came, they were reluctant to imitate the behaviour of the party agents and the League.

Like commentators among other classes, the Chartists failed to see that the 1832 Reform Act created not so much a rigid distinction between the enfranchised and the unenfranchised (though at any one moment there was a line drawn between the two, because either you were on the current electoral register or you were not), as a spectrum. At one end of the spectrum were those with many votes — people like Pye Smith, a wealthy Nonconformist divine, who in virtue of his wealth, not his Nonconformity, had votes in Tower Hamlets, Middlesex, North Staffordshire, North Derbyshire and the West Riding.[46] In the middle came both those with one vote, and those who possessed all but one of the qualifications — men who occupied £50 farms, or £10 houses in the towns, but had not yet occupied them for twelve months previous to 31 July. Beyond them came those who failed to satisfy two of the requirements, but still had grounds to hope that one day they would satisfy all of them, and, further over still, those who had so little hope of ever attaining the franchise that neither they nor the political agents bothered even to reckon the number of qualifications they possessed and the number they lacked. Within this spectrum it was possible for men on one side of the line (as drawn in a particular year) to have undergone the same sort of experiences as had men on the other. The man whose vote had been objected to, who had lost it for one year, and who recovered it the next had something in common with the man whose vote had been objected to and who was without a vote now. Both had something in common, too, with the man whose vote had been objected to and saved at the cost of expense and vexation, and with the man whose claim had been objected to so strenuously that he had given up trying and never reached the register.

It was facts like these which made it conceivable that, if the inconvenience attendant upon the registration ever seriously came to be regarded as intolerable, some of the enfranchised themselves would join the leaders of the unenfranchised in demanding a simplified system, even if it meant an increased electorate and a step towards democracy. We have already seen how, in 1835, the Radical *Manchester and Salford Advertiser* argued that the way to eliminate the insupportable excitement of the registration would be to do away with residence and occupation requirements and, in the boroughs, the requirement to have paid rates and assessed taxes, and to advance to universal (adult male) suffrage.[47] Nine years later the same point was made to the Select Committee on the Votes of Electors when Mr Kynnersley, a revising barrister, was led, through his interrogation, up to the point where he was ready, like previous witnesses, to condemn the manufacture of faggot votes and the electoral tactics of the Anti-Corn Law League, as the committee's sponsors intended. But at this point Milner Gibson, a Reformer, intervened, and put it to him that the best answer to all the annoyances and frustrations in the registration would be to simplify the franchise.[48] Although universal suffrage would not solve everything, for there would still be the problem of excluding aliens and minors, the moral was always there for men to draw, and one reason why Peel and Graham attempted to improve the working of the existing system in 1843 was presumably in order to forestall any attempt by the Complete Suffrage Movement, or any other suffrage movement, to turn the more glaring deficiencies to their own ends.

It was never quite out of the question, then, that an alliance could be formed across the spectrum and for the purposes of Movement. This was something which the modern agitator would not fail to notice and exploit, and which the Chartist leaders themselves seem never to have perceived. Having missed the tactical opportunities offered to them in the 1830s and 1840s, they seem subsequently to have found themselves the victims of a tacit alliance across the spectrum and for the purposes of Resistance in the 1850s. The repeal of the Corn Laws and the distintegration of Peel's party were followed by a rise in living standards and a decline in political skirmishing. Thanks to the institution of a court of appeal, men began to have confidence in the registration procedures, and, finally, as the registration law became more uniform, manuals of registration law proliferated. Cox and Grady's famous *Law and Practice of Registration and Elections* was first published in 1847, and reprinted upon many occasions in the 1850s and 1860s, while A. J. P. Lutwych's authoritative *Reports of Cases Argued and Determined in the Court of Common Pleas on Appeal from the Decisions of the Revising Barristers* appeared in 1854. Everything told in the same direction. The annual revision went more smoothly, because there was less excitement, and as a result there was still less excitement. Rising prosperity was then carrying successive layers of working men up to the boundary with sufficient confidence that, when the time came, registration would be no problem. Those who were below the line began to join those above it in thinking that it was a good franchise in a good system. Men who by diligence at their trades rose to the point on the wage scale where they either did, or could soon expect to, move into a £10 house or purchase a forty-shilling freehold did not want to see the gates opened too wide behind them, and the Chartists were out-manoeuvred.

It is worth emphasising the point that the system settled down, because the one historian since Seymour to look closely at the registration, J. A. Thomas, concluded that the machinery was inefficient, and that the overseers in particular were guilty of incompetence and indifference. Thomas's view has been given wide publicity by Professor Hanham, who asserted that the

overseers were 'totally unqualified', and that by 1870 they had
become a by-word for 'inefficiency, ignorance and illiter-
acy'.[49]

Thomas took his evidence mainly from the reports of two
Select Committees, in 1868—9 and 1870.[50] He did not,
however, make any allowance for the fact that in 1868—9 and
1870 the overseers in both boroughs and counties were strug-
gling to make sense of the new franchises introduced in 1867,
and had twice as much work to do as they had done hitherto. It
was the most unfavourable moment for their reputation — it
was in a sense 1835 all over again — and much of the evidence
taken before the two committees was not relevant to the
immediately preceding period. It might have been fairer to the
registration officials to have considered that in the 1850s, when
both Russell and Disraeli toyed with the notion of fancy
franchises, all sorts of objections were raised against the proposal, but that one objection which does not seem to have been
raised, in Parliament at any rate, was that it would be impossible, or even unduly complicated, to register them.

Nobody would wish to argue that the registration system was
perfect in the 1850s or at any other time. In the boroughs it
still suffered from one glaring deficiency, which was its failure
to cater for the compound householder — the tenant who paid
his rates through his landlord, and whose name remained
unknown, therefore, to the overseers. As we have seen, the Act
of 1832 had included a provision conferring upon the tenant
the right to demand to be allowed to pay the rates in person.[51]
But in many areas tenants generally seem to have preferred to
suppose that their landlords were 'paying' the rates, and even
the minority of tenants who were not afraid to jeopardise their
relations with their landlords by making the demand were
deterred by the necessity to repeat it every year. Accordingly,
in 1851, the law was changed by Clay's Act,[52] to save the
tenant trouble by allowing him, after making the demand once,
to retain the qualification as long as he continued to occupy the
same house and to pay the rates. But the lethargy of potential
electors was not to be overcome so easily, and in 1866
Gladstone declared that, to the best of his belief, not even one
in fifty of the 40,000 compound householders in London had
availed himself of Clay's Act.[53] The problem of the compound
householder remained unsolved, and in due course played a

prominent part in the debates preceding and succeeding the second Reform Act.[54]

The compound householder apart, contemporaries agreed, almost universally, that the 'automatic' system of registration in the boroughs was superior to that in the counties. In so far as registration procedures remained a live issue in the 1850s and early 1860s it was the counties which kept them so, and the one further Select Committee which was appointed in this period to inquire into the registration was confined to the counties by its terms of reference. This committee of 1864 heard and rehearsed all the old complaints. 'Persons entitled to a vote are liable to be annually called upon to substantiate their right', and suffer 'annoyance and expense'. Speculative 'objections are ventured [by party agents] on the chance that the persons objected to will be unable or unwilling to take up the challenge, and will thus forfeit their votes', and 'great facilities are afforded for placing or continuing upon the register of a county the names of persons not qualified to vote'. The committee, like its predecessor in 1846, was attracted by the possibility of making the registration of voters in the English counties a matter of 'official agency', in the same way as it was in the English boroughs and in the constituencies in Scotland.[55] Like its predecessor, too, it came to the reluctant conclusion that the nature and variety of the qualifications for the county franchise 'limit the application of any official system' and made it impossible to do what everyone agreed was desirable.[56] In the last resort the county Members and their supporters always closed ranks against any suggestion which might have broken the secrecy surrounding the ownership of property. Gentlemen were not prepared to lay their title deeds, and farmers their leases, before the overseers, and the Select Committee therefore ended up by recommending a series of minor and very detailed modifications to the registration procedures, embodied in the County Voters Act of 1865,[57] which threw doubt upon the intolerable nature of the evils of which they complained.

No further major changes, then, were made or needed to be made in the registration law between 1843 and 1867, and the result was that everyone connected with its operation, the political parties, the revising barristers and the overseers, had the opportunity to grow into the system. The political parties began to learn how to behave if they were to enjoy the respect

of the public and become an accepted part of the legitimate
constitutional scene; the revising barristers' visits to the constituencies became part of the calendar of the year; and the
overseers, too, in the vast majority of cases, became adequate to
the role for which they had been cast. The incompetent and
politically biased overseer was not the rule. One witness before
the 1846 committee said that overseers generally were com-
petent, but that 'a great number' were incompetent, and this
may have been as close as one could have got to an accurate
summary of the position at that time.[58] Fourteen years later a
witness before a Select Committee of the House of Lords,
appointed to inquire into the probable increase in the number
of electors from a lowering of the qualification for the franchise, drew an important distinction between the assistant (i.e.
paid) overseers employed in the large parishes, who were very
superior persons, and the great mass of overseers, who were not
very intelligent men.[59] Even in the country districts, however,
it was held both in 1860 and in 1864 that 'the overseers are the
parties who have the best means of forming a judgement' and
that the business was now so well understood that it would be
unwise to make any changes.[60] The average standard was
passable, and in areas like Lancashire (as opposed, perhaps, to
large towns like Liverpool), where there seems to have been no
difficulty in finding men of polished educational attainments,
the overseers behaved impeccably. When Mr Hulton, the clerk
of the peace for Lancashire, with twenty-five years experience
of the registration, was asked by the Select Committee of 1884
what happened if the overseers neglected their duty and did not
return the lists, he replied simply that the question never arose,
because 'the overseers always do return the lists'.[61] The
negligent overseer was a rarity, and, in writing about the
registration system in general and the overseers in particular,
Thomas and Hanham mistook the time the machine spent at the
garage being serviced for the time it spent on the open road.
Neither went beyond the reports of Select Committees which
were appointed to find out what was wrong, to the registers
themselves, which were laboriously and faithfully compiled,
year by year, in accordance with the Acts of 1832 and 1843,
for every constituency in the land. Nobody who consults the
registers can doubt the general truth of Cobden's judgement
when he contrasted the situation in 1844 with the state of affairs

before 1832, and argued that 'It will not do now, as it did under the old system, to create fictitious votes': 'you must have a *bona fide* qualification', 'there is now a register, there was none formerly'.[62] Had it been otherwise, the overseers and the revising barristers would not have been retained at each successive Reform Act until 1918, by which time the whole basis of the overseers' existence in relation to the treatment of poverty was disappearing. The function of preparing the lists was then taken over by the town clerks in the boroughs and the clerks of the peace in the counties.

With both the electorate and the registration officials settling down, interest in the system remained, for much of the 1850s and 1860s, at a rather academic level, and was concerned mainly with the collection of statistics. Following the first census, in 1801, statistics about the population were published every ten years throughout the nineteenth century; but no provision was made in the Reform Act of 1832 for the Registrar General to collect and publish electoral statistics, which could easily have been handed in by the revising barristers, or forwarded by the returning officers and the clerks of the peace, year by year. Nevertheless, usable statistics were published for each of the English boroughs and counties for twenty-three years out of the thirty-six between 1832 and 1867, though not for exactly the same years in the counties as in the boroughs. These are set out in Table 1.

It is worth asking where the statistics came from. A Select Committee could ask for statistics to be prepared, and a Minister of the Crown could ask for a return upon his own authority. Thus the Select Committee on election expenses secured the statistics relating to 1833, Lord John Russell laid the figures for the 1853 registration before Parliament in order to facilitate the progress of the Reform Bill in 1854, Mr Clive, Under-Secretary at the Home Department, published figures for the number of registered electors in the boroughs in 1859, in time for the debate upon the Reform Bill of 1860, and the President of the Poor Law Board prepared the statistics required for the discussion of the Reform Bill in 1866. But the remainder of the statistics which were collected and published were entirely the result of unofficial action and of private

TABLE 1

Prime Sources of Electoral Statistics

Boroughs		Called for by
1832 in PP	1833 XXVII 21	Mr J. Hume
1833	1834 IX 604	Select Committee
1834	1836 XLIII 373	Mr J. S. Wortley
1835	1836 XLIII 421	Mr D. W. Harvey
1836	1837–8 XLIV 553	Mr J. Hume
1839	1840 XXXIX 187	Mr J. Hume
1840	1843 XLIV 117	Mr H. G. R. Yorke
1842	1844 XXXVIII 427	Mr J. Hume
1846	1847 XLVI 335	Mr William Williams
1847	1849 XLV 175	Sir Benjamin Hall*
1848	1850 XLVI 199	Mr F. H. F. Berkeley
1849	1850 XLVI 199	Mr F. H. F. Berkeley
1850	1852 XLII 309	Sir Thomas Birch and Sir Benjamin Hall
1851	1852 XLII 309	Sir Benjamin Hall
1852	1852–3 LXXXIII 409	Sir Fitzroy Kelly
1853	1854 LIII 219	Lord John Russell
1856	1857 (2) XXXIV 83	Mr Locke King
1858	1859 XXIII 139	Mr T. S. Western
1859	1860 LV 57	Mr G. Clive
1860	1862 XLIV 703	Mr C. N. Newdegate
1862	1864 XLVIII 227	Mr Locke King
1863	1864 XLVIII 227	Mr Locke King
1865	1866 LVII 235	Mr Lambert of the Poor Law Board

In addition some figures for 1837 are in PP (Parliamentary Papers) 1837–8 XLIV 553, for 1855 in PP 1857 XXXIV 83, and for 1857 in PP 1859 XXIII 129.

Counties	in PP	Called for by
1832		Mr J. Hume
1833	XXVII 21	Select Committee
1834	IX 602	Mr J. S. Wortley
1835	XLIII 373	Anonymous
1836	XLIII 363	Mr J. Hume
1836	1837–8 XLIV 553	Mr J. Hume
1839	XXXIX 187	Mr J. Hume
1842	1844 XXXVIII 427	Mr H. Elphinstone
1845	1846 XXXIII 145	Mr William Williams
1846	XLVI 335	Mr F. H. F. Berkeley
1848	XLVI 199	Mr F. H. F. Berkeley
1849	XLVI 199	Sir Benjamin Hall
1850	XLII 309	Sir Benjamin Hall
1851	XLII 309	Mr Locke King
1852	1857 (2) XXXIV 83	Lord John Russell
1853	1854 LIII 211	Mr Locke King
1854	1857 (2) XXXIV 83	Mr W. Laslett
1855	1857 (1) XIV 533	Mr Locke King
1856	1857 (2) XXXIV 83	Mr T. S. Western
1858	1859 (1) XXIII 139	Mr C. N. Newdegate
1860	1862 XLIV 703	Mr Locke King
1862	1864 XLVIII 227	Mr Locke King
1863	1864 XLVIII 227	Mr J. A. Blake
1864	1865 XLVII 549	

In addition there are some figures for 1837 in *PP* 1837–8 XLIV 553, and for 1867 in *PP* 1867–8 XX 957. Figures in *PP* 1860 LV 85 may refer to 1859.

* For doubts as to the value of this return see below p. 136.

enterprise among individual Members of Parliament, and the interesting point is the character of the persons making the inquiries. Concern for statistics — the very idea that a discussion should begin with the facts — was, right from the start, a Radical characteristic. Even in the 1830s and 1840s, when the Conservative Members might have been expected to move for return after return exhibiting the fact that, in relation to their populations, the counties were grossly under-represented, it was in fact the Radicals who made the running, with inquiries intended to show that the Reform Act had not enfranchised as many persons as had been expected. By the late 1850s, when the Conservatives were at last interested in passing a Reform Act of their own, demography was working against them. The counties were still arguably under-represented, but the county populations had reached, or even passed, their peaks, and the tide of population was running strongly towards the towns.

The electoral statistics for the boroughs, for the twenty-three years listed in Table 1, are contained in twenty reports. Of these, one (1833) was called for by a Select Committee, and three others (1853, 1859 and 1865) by Ministers. Out of the remaining sixteen, three only (1834, 1852 and 1860) were asked for by Conservative MPs, and no fewer than thirteen by Radicals. In the counties the story is much the same. The figures for the twenty-three years are contained in eighteen reports. One report (1835) is not attributed to anyone, one (1833) was called for by a Select Committee, and one (1853) was a Ministerial return. Out of the remaining fifteen returns, two only (1834 and 1860) were moved for by Conservatives, and thirteen by Radicals.

When we widen the field of inquiry to include not just those reports which are of primary statistical use, but, in addition, other reports which called for statistics of registered electors in one form or another, the pattern and the proportions remain the same. On the Conservative side there appear to have been two kinds of person involved in these inquiries. The first group, the bravos, standing to the right of the party, wanted to show that statistics could be made to prove Tory points. Among them were to be found Sir Fitzroy Kelly (East Suffolk), who wished to ascertain the number of persons (primarily the freemen) continuing to enjoy the ancient franchises preserved to them by the Lords' amendments to the 1832 Reform Bill,[63] Packe

(South Leicestershire), who was interested in the number of non-residents polling in the counties,[64] and Hunt (North Northamptonshire), who in 1866 sought to demonstrate how well the working classes were already represented under the existing franchises.[65] The second group, who stood to the left of the party, and were, it could be argued, better Conservatives, took an entirely different line. Accepting the fact that statistics told in favour of Reform, they sought to deny the Radicals a monopoly both of the Reform issue and of the inquiries upon which demands for Reform could be based. Thus Lord Robert Montagu (Huntingdonshire), who favoured moderate Parliamentary reform, Long (Chippenham), who would admit the steady sober portion of the working men to the franchise, and Newdegate (North Warwickshire), who liked it to be known that he 'could not be taunted with objecting to the admission of the working classes to the franchise as he and others had founded a freehold land society . . . with the express object of enabling working men to obtain a property qualification', were all trying to make the point that, if there had to be another Reform Act, there was really no reason why the Conservatives should not pass one themselves.[66]

On the Radical side matters were even more clear-cut. In the 1830s it had been Joseph Hume, critic of government extravagance and jealous guardian of the people's purse, who had made the running. He was joined or followed by Harvey (Colchester), a Whig inclined to Radicalism; Yorke (York), 'a moderate Reformer where moderation is sufficient . . . a radical Reformer, when radicalism is best, but above all things, an uncompromising friend of the people'; Williams, who was the Member for Coventry, the most 'popular' constituency in the country; Ayrton, Berkeley, Sir Thomas Birch, Sir Benjamin Hall, and Locke, all of whom sat for large constituencies (Tower Hamlets, Bristol, Liverpool, Marylebone and Southwark); Bright (Birmingham) and Villiers (Wolverhampton), the second- and third-ranking speakers in the Anti-Corn Law League, and Smith (Stockport) its first chairman; Collier (Plymouth), Sir Charles Douglas (Banbury), Elphinstone (Lewes), Laslett (Worcester), Western (Maldon), and White (Brighton), all of whom favoured both Parliamentary reform and the introduction of the secret ballot; Locke King (E. Surrey), who pinned his Parliamentary career upon the equalisation of the county and borough franchises; and Blake (Waterford), who voted in favour even of Lord Derby's Reform Bill in 1859.[67] Many of these names speak for themselves, and, when we consider that twelve out of these twenty men also drew attention in Dod's *Parliamentary Companion* to the fact that they were in favour of anything from the abolition of church rates to the disestablishment of the Church of England and the redistribution of church revenues, while the remainder, with the exception of Blake, whose interests lay in Ireland, seem to have missed few opportunities of speaking and voting upon these contentious issues, we can see how 'dangerous' the sort of man who was interested in statistics was. Finally, when we notice how an inquiry the results of which might lead to a Conservative conclusion (like Mr Knightley's request for figures showing the number of registered electors entitled to vote for knights of the shire in respect of freehold property situated in any borough that returned Members) was followed at the appropriate moment by a request for information contrasting the number of persons living in large boroughs, and so qualified, with the (far greater) number who qualified to serve on county juries,[68] we shall conclude that they were not only 'dangerous' but vigilant, and that the Chartists who dismissed them so lightly did the middle-class Radicals in Parliament less than justice.

In May 1837 Peel encouraged his supporters to 'Register! Register! Register!' and in November 1838 he wrote that the registration was 'a perfectly new element of political power . . . a more powerful one than either the Sovereign', who had appointed Peel Prime Minister for the first time in 1834, 'or the House of Commons', which had sent Peel back to the opposition benches in 1835.[69] Henceforth that party would be the stronger which had the existing registration in its favour.

Peel did not go on to speculate, after the manner of a political scientist or constitutional historian, exactly where that supreme power lay: whether it resided in the overseers, who drew up the draft lists, the party agents, who lodged claims and objections, the revising barristers, who determined the claims, the senior judges on each circuit, who appointed the revising barristers, or in the appointment of the judges by the Crown.

What was clear, however, was that in the finely balanced state of parties which existed in 1838, any advantage, anywhere along the line, might prove decisive, determine the result of the next general election and, as Peel put it, 'the disposal of offices'. It was a situation which did much to reveal, to a wider public, the continuing importance, in England as in Ireland, of executive appointments. However often Ministers of the Crown, judges, revising barristers, magistrates, and even overseers acted impartially, the fact remained that they were always in a position not to do so. To the extent that Peel was right in thinking that the location of the supreme power in the state was now to be found in the annual registration, so the party activists can be forgiven for thinking that supreme power in the state lay with the administration which appointed the successive grades of registration officials. In that sense the tenure of power came to be seen (as it had been in the bad old days of royal influence) as self-perpetuating. Hence the desperate excitement to regain power when it had been lost, by the Tories in 1832–4 and 1835–41, and by the Reformers in 1834–5 and 1841–6.

There can be little doubt that, despite the Whigs' built-in advantage in the prerogative appointments, between 1837 and 1841 Peel had the better of the struggle to recover power through the constituencies. He continued to hold the initiative right up to 1843, when he passed the new Registration Act (Peel's Political Relations Act?), and even to 1844, when, through the medium of the Bank Charter Act, he restricted the money supply, kept house values down, and effectively closed the door to any possible addition of the working classes to the borough electorate through the operation of inflation.

But Peel's victory at the general election of 1841 set the Reformers' minds working. The Chandos Clause provided an explanation of and an excuse for their defeat, and a huge potential array of urban freeholders lay ready, waiting to be mobilised, to mount a counter-attack. Professor Moore has argued that the Whigs who framed the Reform Bill of 1831 wished to separate the boroughs from the counties and to restore the influence of traditional local nexus.[70] His argument rests upon a single clause in the original Bill, which would have prevented the urban freeholder, resident or non-resident, in respect of whose property either he or his tenant could claim a vote in the borough, from registering a vote in the county. Certainly this indicates an intention to separate the boroughs from the counties to some extent, and it may be that some degree of restoration of the traditional structure of the constituencies was one of the things the Whigs had in mind.

But, even if we look at the urban freeholder in the way Professor Moore would like us to, it is worth noticing (as indeed Professor Moore himself does), that the original clause would not have excluded the many urban freeholders whose properties were worth less than a £10 house and more than a forty-shilling freehold from voting in the counties.[71] The separation envisaged would never, therefore, have been absolute, and the original clause was later amended, following the Cabinet's decision not to oppose the Chandos Clause, which would allow a farmer and his landlord in the county to vote in respect of the same property, to allow the non-resident urban freeholder, whose tenant would in future claim a vote in the borough, to continue himself to vote in the county in respect of the same property.[72] If we are to attribute the outcome not to contingent factors, the press of debate and the desire for equity, but to a settled intention upon the part of the framers of the Act, then it would appear more probable that the Whigs, who never entertained the simple solution, which would have been to draw a rigid line between the borough and county electorates, were content to leave both the counties and the boroughs with some interest in and hold over each other. It was notorious how many houses in the smaller boroughs were owned by county families, who expected their borough tenants, like their farm tenants, to vote as they were told; and the Whigs, who, if they possessed an ideology, expressed it in their dislike of absolutes — absolute monarchs, absolute democracies, absolute identification of the counties with the Tories and the boroughs with the Reformers — were, not surprisingly, content to see the boroughs retain a foothold in the affairs of the counties.

Politics were not primarily about the cultivation of local nexus, important though these were to most Tories and many Whigs. Politics were to decide who were to hold the great offices of state and to take the initiative in legislation, and politicians were organised in parties, and to a remarkable extent, in the 1830s, in two parties. Whether this was what the Whigs intended or not, tension between the parties was channelled by the Reform Act into the registration and the annual revision. And, when the Tories were believed to have triumphed through the Chandos Clause, the Reformers fought back through the urban freeholders at the points where urban and rural interests met — wherever, in short, a populous town faced a proud county. The party activists on both sides may have been a tiny minority, operating in a relatively small number of constituencies, but three times, in 1835, in 1840 and in 1845, and in three very different ways, the party activists were able to turn the registration into the leading issue in politics. Unless one sees this, one will, like Professor Moore, miss some of the significance of the strong feelings aroused both by the attempts to register and by the attempts to frustrate the registration of Nonconformist ministers, of the new Registration Act of 1843, and of the tens of thousands of objections made by the League in 1845, and one will be tempted to interpret the judges' decision in the case of Alexander *v.* Newman as a violation of the intentions of the Reformers of 1832,[73] and to be misled by Peel's thorough drainage scheme into supposing that the repeal of the Corn Laws was also, like the Reform Act, a cure rather than a concession.[74]

Viewed from a standpoint which assumes that political warfare has its base in the constituencies and its front line in Parliament and the executive offices of state, and recognises the role of party in connecting the two, the entire period between 1832 and 1847 can be interpreted as one continuous registration battle, which Peel joined in when he appreciated its importance, and then lost. Peel surrendered in 1845–6, as soon as he saw the battle turning against him, without giving the constituency agents on his own side the chance to fight back against the League and with the League's own weapons. This neglect embittered even his most fervent admirers, and the conflict which followed between the two wings of the former Conservative party placed the initiative in Parliament and the command of the executive back in the hands of the Reformers. Fortunately for the Tories, the League was wound up, Cobden himself was less than wholehearted in his support for the Freehold Land Societies, and the Chartists proved incapable of taking up the struggle where he slackened off. The consequence was that for nearly twenty years successive Whig governments came under so little external pressure that they were able, in effect, to extend a truce to the Conservatives (and their local nexus) in the counties. Live and let live became the basic pattern of British politics in the middle of the nineteenth century, the Whigs at Westminster and Whitehall, the Tories in the shires. Not until the Tories, under Disraeli, became once again a governing party, would the Reformers, or Liberals, be stimulated to mount a new series of concerted attacks upon the aristocracy and the shires.

Appendix
The Registration Returns

The statistics suffer from a number of imperfections and should be used with caution. In addition to the well-known problems concerning the uneven values of house and farm property in different parts of the country, and the difficulties with double entries, there were a number of factors operating in Westminster and Whitehall which mean that the whole do not, as Erskine May put it, 'present so regular and complete a series as could be desired'.[1]

The procedure was for a Member to approach the Minister whose department would have to secure the information — in this case usually the Home Office — and, having obtained his agreement, to move for a return. Ministers were obliging, and motions for returns were not normally opposed. The officers of the House would then write to the department concerned, and the department would conduct the inquiry through its normal bureaucratic channels. In the case of the Home Office, this meant that the clerks wrote to the returning officers (till 1843) or the town clerks (after 1843) of the boroughs, and to the clerks of the peace in the counties, telling them what was required. These would then make what they could of the questions, and return such answers as they thought fit, and the Home Office would forward the answers to the House of Commons to be printed.

There was room for error and misunderstanding at every stage of this process. The ordinary Member of Parliament knew nothing of the machinery he was setting in motion, and did not understand that anyone need be taught to use it. The result was that all too often the input to the 'machine' was a badly phrased question, or even one which a number of constituencies could not answer. There was, and to this day still is, almost infinite scope for confusion in the dates of the registers, because each new register came into force on 1 November (from 1843, 1 December) and lasted for one year. Thus, when, for example, Sir Benjamin Hall asked, in 1849, for a return of the number of registered electors in each borough and city 'in 1847', and the number polled at the last general election, some constituencies interpreted this to mean the register in force for the greater part of 1847 and upon which the general election of 1847 was fought (i.e. the register compiled in 1846), and others the register compiled in 1847, which came into force four months after the election. Faced with a return of this kind, the Home Office lacked either the resources or the resourcefulness to edit it. A figure, even if it obviously related to the wrong year, or was grotesque, was a figure. Let it pass.

It is difficult to resist the conclusion that the Home Office clerks did not put their hearts into the prosecution of what were, from their point of view, peripheral inquiries upon behalf of Members of Parliament. MPs, after all, came and went, while the Home Office went on for ever, and had much to lose by pressing inquiries upon local officials whose goodwill it depended upon for the smooth running of the normal business of the department.[2] Some constituencies appear never to have been asked to supply the information required – Marlborough appears to have been omitted from the first two inquiries in 1832 and 1833, while the Isle of Wight, which featured in these, appears to have been omitted from the next six inquiries, between 1834 and 1846. Some of the constituencies which were written to made no return, and in these cases the clerks appear to have been content, for many years, to enter 'no return' upon their papers. Even when they did take a more serious view of their responsibilities, and make 'repeated applications' for information, they had no power to compel its production (though the House of Commons had). Finally, when the returns came in, the office seems to have had no settled procedure for setting them out in alphabetical order, and it took a generation and more to establish the convention that the county of Southampton was called Hampshire South, while the names of boroughs like Kingston upon Hull, St Ives and Chipping Wycombe were a recurrent source of alphabetical confusion.

As time went by these defects became apparent. The Printing Committee of the House of Commons appreciated that returns were being asked for without any plan or principle. Too little care and thought were given to the formulation of the questions, to the preparation of instructions to those responsible for answering them, to the checking of returns as they came in, and to the need, in cases of doubt, to ask for confirmation. Accordingly, in 1841 the committee suggested that, before giving notice of a motion for a return, every Member should consult the Librarian of the House of Commons in order to ascertain the manner in which previous returns were compiled and the ways in which their defects might be remedied. The Librarian himself was to take a hand in the drafting of the forms of inquiry, and in the editing of the answers before they were printed.[3] No doubt these recommendations effected some improvement, but as late as 1860 a Member asking for the number of registered electors in each constituency 'for the year 1858' and the number who voted 'at the last General Election', received figures relating to the register of 1858 upon which the election of 1859 was fought — the register of 1857, which was in force for the greater part of 1858 — and even, in some constituencies where there had been no contest in 1859, for the register of 1856, upon which the contest at the general election of 1857 had been fought.[4]

As far as possible, then, the published returns should always be checked against the original registers, where these have survived. But here we encounter another difficulty. For a long time, now, historians have made use of the census reports and of street directories. More recently they have paid a lot of attention to poll books. But so little use has so far been made of the registers of Parliamentary electors that some archivists scarcely know which lists they have. In these circumstances it is too early to attempt to publish a list of the registers which have survived. But the objective will be worth pursuing. The information contained in the registers is restricted when compared with that to be found in the census reports, but it was at least collected every year.

We know from the manner in which they were constructed that the county registers suffer both from dead wood and from omissions. We may suspect that they monitor the activity of party agents (though this is worth recording), and we may anticipate that they will serve mainly as a general guide to the rapid growth of the electorate in 1835, to the stagnation in the numbers of tenants at will in the 1840s and 1850s, and to the remarkable stability of the county electorate throughout the whole period between the first and second Reform Acts. For these reasons there may not be much to be learned by going to the archives in order to fill in the gaps in the officially published statistics and to form a series.

On the other hand, there can be little doubt that, in the boroughs, and especially in the boroughs listed on schedules C and D of the Reform Act of 1832, where there were no ancient franchises and every elector was a £10 householder, the variations in the numbers of £10 householders able to keep up to date with the payment of their rates and assessed taxes do provide us with a measure of the fluctuations of the economy. As Table 2 shows, the published figures reveal a marked setback in Lancashire in 1848, consequent, presumably, upon the scarcity of cotton and the financial crisis of 1847. The figures for the Black Country, on the other hand, strongly suggest that the recession did not affect the iron trades in the same way. The widespread nature of the recession in 1847 does, however, show up in the figures for London, for all the boroughs on Schedule C and for all the boroughs on Schedule D.

It seems reasonable to suppose, therefore, that it will be worthwhile going to the archives to try to fill in the whole

TABLE 2
Registered Electors in Boroughs Listed in Schedules C and D of the Reform Act of 1832

	Lancashire and Cheshire	Black Country	London	Schedule C	Schedule D
1842	21,134	10,183	56,656	103,420	16,656*
1846	25,255	11,246	69,403	122,194	18,442
1847	25,390	11,988	71,457	124,648	18,618
1848	23,844	12,214	70,828	123,905	17,630
1849	24,175	12,442	79,205	132,408	18,344

* Merthyr estimated at 776.

Note: Part of the increase in 1849 must be attributed to the Act of 1848 (11 and 12 Vict. c. 90), which changed the law in such a way as to require the borough voter to have paid by 20 July the rates due from him up to the previous 5 January — giving him an extra three months grace.

series, and especially, perhaps, to try to fill in the gap between 1839 and 1842, when the economy suffered its most serious and its most complicated dislocation in the whole century between 1815 and 1914. It should be possible, for example, to establish from the electoral registers whether this was a simple depression or a double-troughed one. It should be possible, too, to draw significant conclusions about the fortunes of individual towns. But there are many local factors at work in a constituency (and in a record office), and the value of micro-studies in the registration still remains to be proved. What is certain is that anyone who examines the original registers in either the counties or the boroughs, together with the accounts of the annual revisions printed in the newspapers, will discover all sorts of unexpected social relationships and party animosities, and a complex world of legal niceties.

Notes

PD is *Parliamentary Debates*. PP is *Parliamentary Papers*. In PP references, the page numbers cited are those of the relevant volume, not the original page numbers of individual reports bound up in the volume.

The place of publication of books is London, unless otherwise stated.

CHAPTER 1

1. *PD* 3 ser. LVI 928, 23 Feb 1841.
2. 3 Geo. III c.15.
3. A. C. Wood, *A History of Nottinghamshire* (Nottingham, 1947) p. 297; A. Temple Patterson, *Radical Leicester, a History of Leicester 1780–1850* (Leicester, 1954) pp. 146–7.
4. Lord Nugent, *PD* 2 ser. XIX 870, 22 May 1828.
5. In Lancaster, 3260 out of 4000 freemen were non-resident – M. G. Brock *The Great Reform Act* (1973) p. 24.
6. 7 and 8 William III c. 25.
7. 10 Anne c. 23.
8. 18 Geo. II c. 18, cl. ii.
9. 20 Geo. III c. 17, cl. i.
10. 28 Geo. III c. 36.
11. 29 Geo. III c. 13 and c. 18.
12. *PP* 1826–27 IV 1105–6.
13. 38 Geo. III c. 60.
14. 42 Geo. III c. 116.
15. *PP* 1817 III 70.
16. *PP* 1826–7 IV 1109.
17. Susan Fairlie, 'The Nineteenth Century Corn Law Reconsidered', *Economic History Review*, 1965.
18. *PD* 2 ser. XVI 1188 and 1197, 15 Mar 1827, and 3 ser. X 543, 20 Feb 1832.
19. *PP* 1817 III 69–71, and 1820 II 329–32.
20. *PP* 1826–7 IV 1111–12.
21. Report, *PP* 1826–7 IV 1105–10; Bill, *PP* 1826–7 II 315–42.

22. Lord Lowther, *PD* 2 ser. XVIII 1348, 25 Mar 1828; Col. Wood, *PD* 3 ser. VI 1160, 5 Sep 1831.
23. Althorp, *PD* 2 ser. XVIII 990, 6 Mar 1828.
24. *PP* 1826—7 IV 1106.
25. *PD* 2 ser. XIX 903, 23 May 1828.
26. *PD* 2 ser. XIX 868—72, 22 May 1828.
27. Sir C. Wetherell, Attorney General, *PD* 2 ser. XVIII 1349, 25 Mar 1828.
28. *PD* 2 ser. XVIII 1348, 25 Mar 1828.
29. *PD* 2 ser. XIX 868—9, 22 May 1828.

CHAPTER 2

1. *PD* 3 ser. LXVIII 1093, 1 May 1843.
2. Lord Durham, Lord Duncannon, Sir James Graham, Lord John Russell.
3. The first Bill (March) and the second Bill (June) provided for the county lists to be revised by the barristers and for the borough lists to be revised by the returning officers. The revision of the borough lists was added to the revising barristers' tasks in September 1831.
4. *PD* 3 ser. VI 1161, 5 Sep 1831.
5. 1 Geo. II c. 9.
6. Althorp, *PD* 3 ser. VI 1060, 2 Sep 1831.
7. J. D. Chambers, *An Examination into Certain Errors and Anomalies in the Principles and Detail of the Registration Clauses of the Reform Act, with Suggestions for their Amendment* (1832) pp. 14—15.
8. Ibid., pp. 30—1.
9. *PD* 3 ser. VI 309, 19 Aug 1831.
10. *PD* 3 ser. VI 1050, 2 Sep 1831.
11. Col. Wood (*PD* 3 ser. VI 1048, 2 Sep 1831) and Sir Edward Sugden (*PD* 3 ser. X 83, 8 Feb 1832) raised the point, though not quite in the context in which it is put here.
12. Sugden, *PD* 3 ser. VI 1053, 2 Sep 1831.
13. Baring, *PD* 3 ser. VI 310, 19 Aug 1831.
14. *PD* 3 ser. LXVIII 820, 11 Apr 1843.
15. Sugden, *PD* 3 ser. X 83, 8 Feb 1832.
16. *The League*, 22 Feb 1845, p. 337 (editorial).
17. Ibid., 21 June 1845, p. 609 (editorial).
18. Ibid., 22 Feb 1845, p. 337 (editorial).
19. Idem.
20. Wood, *PD* 3 ser. VI 1049, 2 Sep 1831; Chambers, *An Examination*, p. 30.
21. *PD* 3 ser. X 91, 8 Feb 1832.
22. *PP* 1826—7 IV 1107—8.
23. 2 and 3 William IV c. 45, cl. xxvii.
24. Idem.
25. Ibid., cl. xxx.

26. Lord Eliot, *PD* 3 ser. LXXIII 1702, 1 Apr 1844.
27. *PP* 1847 XLVI 333—46.
28. 2 and 3 William IV c. 45, cl. li.
29. Ibid., cl. xliv.
30. Ibid., cl. xlvi.
31. Ibid., cl. xliv.
32. Ibid., cl. xlvii.
33. Ibid., cl. l.
34. Ibid., cl. liv.
35. Ibid., cl. xviii—xx.
36. *PP* 1846 VIII 378 (3306).
37. 2 and 3 William IV c. 45, cl. xxvi.
38. Idem.
39. Ibid., cl. xviii.
40. In view of the long connection between the county franchise and the
     land tax, cl. xxii specifically excluded the necessity for an elector to
     be assessed to the land tax.
41. Ibid., cl. xxxviii—xliii.

CHAPTER 3

1. Pigot, *PD* 3 ser. LIII 63, 25 Mar 1840.
2. *PP* 1836 XLIII 361.
3. *Morning Chronicle*, 28 Oct 1835.
4. *Western Luminary*, 28 Sep 1835.
5. Sir William Follett, *Surrey Standard*, 24 Oct 1835.
6. N. Gash, *Sir Robert Peel* (1972) p. 101.
7. John Prest, *Lord John Russell* (1972) p. 86.
8. Bonham to Peel, British Museum Add. MS. 40420, f. 126, 4 May
    1835.
9. J. K. Buckley, *Joseph Parkes of Birmingham* (1926) p. 129.
10. Bills of 1834, *PP* 1834 II 163—204; of 1835, *PP* 1835 II 583—624.
11. *Birmingham Advertiser*, 24 Sep 1835.
12. *Morning Chronicle*, 29 Sep, and *County Chronicle*, 5 Oct 1835.
13. *Hereford Journal*, 7 Oct 1835.
14. *PP* 1846 VIII 380 (3324).
15. *Morning Chronicle*, 18 Sep, and *Birmingham Advertiser* 17 Sep
     1835.
16. *PP* 1836 XLIII 361.
17. *Hampshire Advertiser*, 17 Oct; *Morning Chronicle*, 20 Oct; *Surrey
     Standard*, 7 Nov; *Norfolk Chronicle*, 10 Oct; *Norwich Mercury*, 10
     Oct; *Western Luminary*, 2 Nov; *The Standard* 10 Oct; *Leeds
     Intelligencer*, 24 Oct 1835.
18. *Norfolk Chronicle*, 3 Oct; *Staffordshire Advertiser*, 3 Oct; and *Bury
     and Norwich Post*, 7 Oct 1835.
19. *Morning Chronicle*, 4 Nov 1835.
20. Gash, *Sir Robert Peel*, p. 101.
21. Figures in *PP* 1834 IX 604—8 (subtract Welsh boroughs), and 1844

XXXVIII 436.

22. Based on my addition of figures for each county in *PP* 1833 XXVII 21—107, and 1836 XLIII 363—67 and 373—80. Figure for 1864 in *PP* 1865 XLIV 551.

23. Lambton MSS., Parkes to Durham, 15 Oct 1837.

24. *PP* 1840 XXXIX 188—90 (my addition).

25. *PD* 3 ser. VI 278—87, 18 Aug 1831.

26. The examples are taken from the S. Warwickshire register of 1832 and the W. Sussex register of 1845.

27. 76,827 out of 396,967 in the counties which made returns (*PP* 1852 XLII 307). See also T. J. Nossiter, *Influence, Opinion and Political Idioms in Reformed England, Case Studies from the North East 1832—1874* (Hassocks, 1975) p. 59.

28. *Hereford Journal*, 7 Oct 1835.

29. *County Herald*, 24 Oct 1835.

30. Ibid., 17 Oct 1835.

31. *Morning Chronicle*, 16 Oct 1835.

32. G. P. Elliott, *A Practical Treatise on the Qualifications and Registration of Parliamentary Electors* (1839) p. 76.

33. *Morning Chronicle*, 4 Nov 1835.

34. *Leeds Intelligencer* and *Manchester Guardian*, 26 Sep 1835.

35. *County Herald*, 17 Oct 1835.

36. *Staffordshire Advertiser*, 3 Oct 1835.

37. See nos 1651, 3493 and 4902 on the Buckinghamshire register for 1832, where the word 'trustee' is included in the qualification.

38. *Norfolk Chronicle*, 3 Oct 1835.

39. *Leeds Intelligencer*, 26 Sep 1835.

40. *Manchester Guardian*, 10 Oct 1835.

41. Idem.

42. *Staffordshire Advertiser*, 3 Oct 1835.

43. *Suffolk Chronicle*, 10 Oct 1835.

44. *Manchester Guardian*, 26 Sep 1835.

45. *Staffordshire Advertiser*, 3 Oct 1835.

46. *Norfolk Chronicle*, 3 Oct 1835.

47. *Manchester Guardian*, 3 Oct 1835, case of Rev. Alfred John Morris.

48. *Morning Chronicle*, 16 Oct 1835.

49. *County Herald*, 24 Oct 1835.

50. *Morning Chronicle*, 13 Oct, and *Norfolk Chronicle*, 3 Oct 1835.

51. *Western Times*, 10 Oct 1835.

52. *Hereford Journal*, 14 Oct 1835.

53. *Western Times*, 17 Oct 1835.

54. *Surrey Standard*, 10 Oct 1835.

55. *Morning Chronicle*, 4 Nov 1835.

56. Ibid., 20 Oct 1835.

57. *Manchester Guardian*, 26 Sep 1835.

58. *Hereford Times*, 3 Oct 1835.

59. *Staffordshire Advertiser*, 3 Oct 1835.

60. *Manchester Guardian*, 3 Oct 1835.

61. J. D. Chambers *The New Bills for the Registration of Electors*

Critically Examined (1836) p. 6.

62. *Morning Chronicle*, 31 Oct 1835.
63. *Surrey Standard*, 10 Oct 1835.
64. *Staffordshire Advertiser*, 3 Oct 1835.
65. Quoted in *Staffordshire Advertiser*, 26 Sep 1835.
66. *Morning Chronicle*, 16 and 17 Sep 1835.
67. *County Herald*, 19 Sep 1835.
68. *Surrey Standard*, 10 Oct 1835.
69. Letter in *Morning Chronicle*, 31 Oct 1836.
70. *Western Luminary*, 19 Oct 1835.
71. *Manchester and Salford Advertiser*, 26 Sep 1835.
72. *Manchester Guardian*, 17 Oct 1835.

CHAPTER 4

1. *Hereford Times*, 10 Oct 1835.
2. *County Herald*, 14 Nov 1835.
3. *Leeds Intelligencer*, 24 Oct 1835.
4. *Leeds Mercury*, 7 Nov 1835.
5. *Surrey Standard*, 10 Oct 1835.
6. *Morning Chronicle*, 5 Nov 1835.
7. Idem.
8. *County Herald*, 26 Sep 1835.
9. *Surrey Standard*, 10 Oct 1835.
10. *Manchester Guardian*, 3 Oct 1835.
11. *Herefordshire Journal*, 7 Oct 1835.
12. *Hereford Times*, 3 and 10 Oct 1835.
13. *Morning Chronicle*, 28 Oct 1835.
14. *County Herald*, 9 May 1835.
15. *Morning Chronicle*, 5 Nov 1835.
16. *PP* 1836 III 385—430.
17. The scheme was floated by Warburton (Bridport) and welcomed by Russell on 20 May (*PD* 3 ser. XXXIII 1134—8).
18. *PD* 3 ser. XXXIV 971, 27 June 1836.
19. *PD* 3 ser. XXXV 907—8, 4 Aug 1836.
20. *Manchester Guardian*, 17 Oct 1835.
21. *Manchester and Salford Advertiser*, 10 Oct 1835.
22. British Museum Add. MS. 40422, ff. 289—92, 8 Dec 1836.
23. *Manchester and Salford Advertiser*, 19 Sep 1835.
24. Ibid., 3 Oct 1835.
25. Lord John Russell, *PD* 3 ser. LVI 238, 2 Feb 1841, and (earlier) LIV 209, 18 May 1840.
26. *Surrey Standard*, 10 Oct. 1835.
27. A. D. Macintyre, *The Liberator* (1965) p. 299.
28. S. Walpole, *Life of Lord John Russell*, 2 vols (1889) vol. 1, p. 132.
29. *PP* 1830 XXIX 461—74.
30. 2 and 3 William IV c. 88.
31. *PP* 1833 XXVII 289—314.

32. Sheil, *PD* 3 ser. LVI 1011–12, 24 Feb 1841.
33. Sheil, *PD* 3 ser. LIV 1332, 19 June 1840.
34. 1 Geo. II c. 9, and 35 Geo. III c. 29.
35. 10 Geo. IV c. 8, and 2 and 3 William IV c. 88.
36. 2 and 3 William IV c. 88, cl. xlvi.
37. Ibid., cl. xxvii.
38. Ibid., cl. xxviii (for the certificate), and 10 Geo. IV c. 8, cl. xxviii (eight years).
39. 2 and 3 William IV c. 88, cl. xxiv, xxv.
40. Stanley, *PD* 3 ser. LIII 126, 26 Mar 1840, and LII 620, 25 Feb 1840.
41. *PD* 3 ser. XXVIII 850, 17 June 1835. The Bill referred to assimilating the registration in Ireland 'as nearly as may be to the Law in force in England and Wales'.
42. 10 Geo. IV c. 8, cl. vi and schedule VI.
43. Plunkett, *PD* 3 ser. XXX 1251, 2 Sep 1835.
44. Stanley, *PD* 3 ser. XLI 881, 13 Mar 1838, and LIII 141, 26 Mar 1840; Sergeant Curry, *PD* 3 ser. LIII 92, 26 Mar 1840.
45. 2 and 3 William IV, c. 88, cl. i, v.
46. See Follett, *PD* 3 ser. LIII 76, 25 Mar 1840; Earl Wicklow, XXX 1253, 2 Sep 1835.
47. *PD* 3 ser. XIV 762, 26 July 1832.
48. Somerville, *PD* 3 ser. LVI 947, 24 Feb 1841.
49. Pigot, *PD* 3 ser. LVI 912, 23 Feb 1841.
50. John C. Alcock, *Registry Cases Reserved for Consideration and Decided by the Twelve Judges of Ireland*, pt 1: Nov 1832 to June 1837 (Dublin, 1837) pp. 55–6.
51. *PP* 1837 XI pt 1, Appendix E.
52. Thomas Welsh, *Registry Cases Comprising All the Published, and Many of the Recent Unpublished, Decisions in Ireland, Respecting the Registration of Voters, under the Irish Reform Act and 10 Geo. IV c. 8* (Dublin, 1840) pp. 126–8.
53. *PP* 1835 II 671–96.
54. Limerick, *PD* 3 ser. XXX 1250, 2 Sep 1835.
55. There are many accounts of this case in the various law reports. I have followed Welsh, *Registry Cases*, pp. 129–48, and Alcock, *Registry Cases*, pp. 55–113.
56. The dates of appointment of the judges were: on the Queen's Bench, Bushe (Chief Justice) 22 Feb 1822, Burton 2 Dec 1820, Crampton 21 Oct 1834, Perrin 31 Aug 1835; at the Common Pleas, Doherty (Chief Justice) 23 Dec 1830, Moore 23 July 1816, Johnson 25 Oct 1817, Torrens 10 July 1823; at the Exchequer, Joy (Chief Baron) 6 Jan 1831, Pennefather 1 Feb 1821, Foster 13 July 1830, Richards 3 Feb 1837. Robert Jebb, *Cases . . . Decided by the Judges of Ireland* (Philadelphia, 1842) pp. ix–x.
57. *PP* 1837 XI.
58. Report in *PP* 1837–8 XIII.
59. Welsh, *Registry Cases*, pp. 211–13.
60. See p. 57 above.
61. *PP* 1837–8 III 682 said that henceforth certificates should not be

necessary but that the elector should obtain one if he wished.

62. *PD* 3 ser. LIII 62—3, 25 Mar (Pigot), and LIV 214, 18 May 1840 (Lord John Russell).

63. O'Connell to O'Brien, 5 and 13 Apr and 29 June 1839, O'Brien Papers, National Library of Ireland.

64. *PD* 3 ser. LII 615—28, 25 Feb 1840.

65. Sergeant Curry, *PD* 3 ser. LIII 92, 26 Mar 1840.

66. Somerville, *PD* 3 Ser. LVI 949, 24 Feb 1841, and LIV 182, 18 May 1840.

67. Somerville, *PD* 3 ser. LIV 186, 18 May 1840.

68. Milnes Gaskell, *PD* 3 ser. LIV 403, 20 May 1840.

69. *PD* 3 ser. LIII 146—7, 26 Mar (O'Connell), LIV 1079, 11 June (Warburton), and LIV 188—9, 18 May 1840 (Grattan).

70. The analysis which follows was prepared by Mrs Angela Aitchison.

71. Kinsale, *PP* 1837—8 XII 1—226, and Carlow borough, *PP* 1839 VI.

72. See *The Times*, 11 June 1840 (Ainsworth to the Mayor of Bolton); and *Dublin Evening Mail*, 10 Mar 1841 (Ainsworth's letter to his constituents).

73. *PD* 3 ser. LIV 357 (Wood), and LIV 368—9 (Howick), 19 May 1840.

74. *PD* 3 ser. LV 459, 6 July 1840.

75. *Morning Chronicle*, 3 July 1840 (O'Connell to Ray, 28 June 1840).

76. *PD* 3 ser. LIV 440, 20 May 1840.

77. *Morning Chronicle* 3 July 1840, 23 Feb 1841; *Dublin Evening Post*, 13 Feb 1841.

78. *Dublin Evening Mail*, 26 Feb 1841.

79. Peel, *PD* 3 ser. LIV 439, 20 May 1840.

80. *The Times*, 28 Mar 1840.

81. Morpeth, *PD* 3 ser. LIV 450, 20 May 1840.

82. *PD* 3 ser. LIII 148, 26 Mar 1840.

83. *Dublin Evening Mail*, 30 Mar 1840.

84. *Morning Chronicle*, 15 June 1840.

85. Extract in *Morning Chronicle*, 3 July 1840.

86. *The Times*, 11 June 1840.

87. Appeals were made to the constituents of Brabazon and Butler in the *Dublin Evening Post* of 8 Apr 1840 (O'Connell's address to the people of the counties of Mayo and Kilkenny, letter 1), to those of Brabazon, Butler and Fitzgibbon in the issue of 10 Apr 1840 (O'Connell's address, letter 2), to those of Howard in the issue of 18 Feb 1841, and to those of Macnamara in the issue of 14 Apr 1840.

88. *The Times*, 11 June 1840.

89. *PD* 3 ser. LII 615—28, 25 Feb 1840.

90. *PD* 3 ser. LIV 399—401, 20 May (Redington), LIV 187, 18 May (Somerville), and LIII 98—9, 26 Mar 1840 (Warburton).

91. *PD* 3 ser. LIV 433, 20 May 1840.

92. *PP* 1840 II 465—70.

93. *PP* 1840 II 509—40.

94. *PP* 1840 II 403—48.

95. *PP* 1840 II 465—70.

96. Lord John Russell, *PD* 3 ser. LIII 1206—7, 4 May 1840.

97. *PP* 1841 XX 555, 615.
98. *PD* 3 ser. LVI 293—4, 4 Feb 1841.
99. *PP* 1841 III 277—322.
100. *PP* 1841 III 323—362.
101. Sir Charles Wood, *PD* 3 ser. LVI 823, 22 Feb 1841, confirmed in *PP* 1837—8 XIII pt 2, 294 (13,109).
102. Morpeth, *PD* 3 ser. LVI 291—2, 4 Feb 1841.
103. *Dublin Evening Mail*, 24 Feb 1841.
104. Morpeth, *PD* 3 ser. LVII 970, 22 Apr 1841.
105. Ebrington to Russell, 19 Apr 1841, Russell Papers, Public Record Office 30. 22. 4A.
106. *The Times*, 28 Mar 1840.

CHAPTER 5

1. To Mrs Arbuthnot, 8 Nov 1838; quoted in C. S. Parker, *Sir Robert Peel*, 3 vols (1891—8) vol. 2, p. 368.
2. *PP* 1842 IV 55—102.
3. 6 and 7 Vict. c. 18.
4. 8 Geo. V c. 64, part 2.
5. 6 and 7 Vict. c. 18, cl. iii and x.
6. Ibid., cl. li and xlvi.
7. Ibid., cl. xvii and schedule B form of notice no. 11.
8. Ibid., cl. c.
9. Sir E. B. Sugden, *PD* 3 ser. LVI 745, 19 Feb 1841.
10. 6 and 7 Vict. c. 18, cl. xlii and lx.
11. Ibid., cl. xxviii; Graham, *PD* 3 ser. LXVII 1084, 17 Mar 1843.
12. 6 and 7 Vict. c. 18, cl. xlix.
13. *PP* 1844 XXXVIII 430 (my addition).
14. 2 and 3 William IV c. 45, cl. xxviii and xxix.
15. 6 and 7 Vict. c. 18, cl. lxxiii.
16. Ibid., cl. lxxxi.
17. Ibid., cl. lxxiv.
18. *PD* 3 ser. LXVII 1085, 17 Mar 1843.
19. *PD* 3 ser. LXVIII 1100, 1 May, and LXIX 239—40, 12 May 1843.
20. *PD* 3 ser. LXVIII 330—1, 3 Apr 1843.
21. *PP* 1847 XLVI 336 (my addition).
22. 2661, 2662, 2673 on the register of 1842.
23. 4829, 4830, 4836 and 4837 on the register of 1842.
24. 1286, 1513, 1532, 1989, 2005, 2147, 2251, 2502 on the register of 1842.
25. 2494 on register of 1842.
26. *The League*, 3 Jan 1846, p. 193 (editorial). H. G. Jordan 'The Political Methods of the Anti-Corn Law League' *Political Science Quarterly*, 1927, pp. 58—76, seems to have come closest to a similar account of the development of the League's tactics.
27. Jordan, in *Political Science Quarterly*, 1927, pp. 65—6.
28. *The League*, 30 Dec 1843, p. 216.

29. Ibid., 30 Sep 1843, p. 5 (Cobden in Covent Garden).
30. Ibid., 4 Nov 1843, p. 81 (editorial).
31. T. J. Nossiter *Influence, Opinion and Political Idioms in Reformed England, Case Studies from the North East 1832—1874*, (Hassocks, 1975) p. 33.
32. *The League*, 25 Nov 1843, p. 129 (editorial).
33. Ibid., 15 June 1844, p. 605 (editorial).
34. Ibid., 25 Jan 1845, p. 276 (council report).
35. Ibid., 6 July 1844, p. 657 (editorial).
36. Ibid., 22 Feb 1845, p. 337 (editorial).
37. Ibid., 1 June 1844, p. 573 (editorial).
38. *PP* 1844 XXXVIII 430 (my addition).
39. *The League*, 15 Nov 1845, p. 86 (Cobden, dinner to Villiers). Cobden later attributed the discovery to Charles Walker of Rochdale; see *Speeches ... by Richard Cobden*, ed. John Bright and J. E. Thorold Rogers, 2 vols (1870) vol. 2, p. 493.
40. *The League*, 23 Nov 1844, p. 132 (Cobden at Rochdale).
41. Ibid., 25 Jan 1845, p. 276 (Great Aggregate Meeting).
42. Ibid., 14 Dec 1844, p. 183 (Cobden).
43. Idem.
44. Ibid., 22 Nov 1845, p. 97 (editorial).
45. Ibid., 10 Feb 1844, p. 313 (editorial).
46. Ibid., 9 Nov 1844, p. 97 (editorial).
47. *PP* 1830—1 II 199 (Mar), and 1831 III 13, cl. xviii (June).
48. 2 and 3 William IV c. 45, cl. xxiv.
49. R. Gibbs, *History of Aylesbury* (Aylesbury, 1885) pp. 276—7.
50. *The League*, 22 Feb 1845, p. 337, (editorial).
51. Ibid., 1 Mar 1845, p. 353 (editorial).
52. *Birmingham Advertiser*, 20 Nov 1845; *The League* 15 Nov 1845, p. 86 (Cobden, dinner to Villiers).
53. *The League*, 28 Sep 1844, p. 1 (editorial).
54. Ibid., 23 Nov 1844, p. 132 (Cobden at Rochdale).
55. Ibid., 30 Nov 1844, p. 145 (editorial).
56. Ibid., 15 Nov 1845, p. 86 (Cobden, dinner to Villiers).
57. Ibid., 9 Nov 1844, p. 97 (editorial).
58. *PP* 1846 VIII 398—9 (3470).
59. *PP* 1846 VIII 253 (1105) (Staffordshire), 286 (1823) (Cheshire), 307 (2312) (Leicestershire), 213 (352—56) (Warwickshire), 295 (2061) (Gloucestershire). D. C. Moore, *The Politics of Deference* (Hassocks, 1976) p. 277, following Mr Newdegate, MP for N. Warwickshire (*PD* 3 ser. CV 1193), gives the impression that the League made 143,731 objections. This is an error: the original reference (*PP* 1846 VIII 407—8, Qn. 3567) makes it clear that the League scrutinised the registers of English counties containing 143,731 electors. About one in eleven electors was objected to.
60. *PP* 1846 VIII 407—8 (3567), quoting *The League*, 13 Dec 1845, p. 148 (G. Wilson at Manchester).
61. *Maidstone Journal*, 2 Dec 1845.
62. For example, the *Brighton Guardian*, 31 Dec, and *Durham*

Chronicle, 26 Dec 1845.

63. *The League*, 21 Feb 1846, p. 366 (supplement, League Registration).
64. Ibid., 15 Nov 1845, p. 81 (editorial).
65. Ibid., 21 Feb 1846, p. 366 (supplement, League registration).
66. Ibid., 15 Nov 1845, p. 81 (editorial).
67. *PP* 1846 VIII 336 (2826).
68. *The League*, 16 Nov 1844, p. 113 (editorial).
69. *Leicestershire Mercury*, 3 Jan 1846.
70. *Leicester Chronicle*, 10 Jan 1846.
71. *Hertfordshire Mercury*, 24 Jan 1846.
72. *PP* 1846 VIII 330—1 (2713).
73. *PP* 1846 VIII 424 (3788).
74. E. Foss, *The Judges of England, with Sketches of their Lives 1066—1864* 9 vols (1848—64) vol. 9, p. 285.
75. *Gentleman's Magazine*, II (1846) 199.
76. *The Times*, 8 July 1846.
77. Ibid., 12 July 1849.
78. J. A. Hamilton in L. Stephen and S. Lees (eds.), *The Dictionary of National Biography*, vol. V (1908), pp. 72—3.
79. *The Times*, 5 Nov 1844.
80. *The English Reports*, CXXXV 81—6.
81. *The League*, 22 Feb 1845, p. 337 (editorial).
82. Ibid., 16 Nov 1844, pp. 118—19 (the registration; figure for 1843 confirmed in *PP* 1846 VIII 398 (3470)), and *PP* 1846 XXXIII 145.
83. *PP* 1846 VIII 398 (3470) and 1846 XXXIII 145.
84. *PP* 1844 XXXVIII 430, and 1846 XXXIII 145.
85. Yorkshire: *The League*, 27 Sep 1845, p. 840 (the registration). Middlesex: ibid., 4 Oct 1845, p. 854.
86. *The English Reports*, CXXXV 890.
87. The decision was reported with glee in *The League*, 7 Feb 1846.
88. *PP* 1846 VIII 342 (2932).
89. *PP* 1846 VIII 180.
90. *The English Reports*, CXXXV 896.
91. *Hertfordshire County Press*, 26 Sep 1846.
92. *Durham Chronicle*, 9 Oct 1846.
93. *The League*, 27 Dec 1845, p. 182 (Cobden at Manchester).
94. *Gentleman's Magazine*, II (1846) p. 199.
95. *PP* 1846 VIII 401 (3489).
96. *The League*, 1 Nov, p. 52 (Cobden at Manchester); 6 Sep, p. 790 (extract from *Cheltenham Free Press*); and 11 Oct 1845, p. 6 (extract from *Hants Independent*).
97. A. Prentice, *A History of the Anti-Corn Law League*, 2 vols (1853) vol. 1, p. 179.
98. *Durham Advertiser*, 29 Aug 1845.
99. *The League*, 18 May 1844, p. 548 (S. Lancashire election).
100. *Hertford Mercury and Reformer*, 29 Nov 1845.
101. *The League*, 21 Sep 1844, p. 839 (the registration).
102. *The League*, 11 Oct 1845, p. 6 (the registration).
103. D. Fraser, 'The Poor Law as a Political Institution', in *The New Poor*

Law in the Nineteenth Century, ed. D. Fraser (1976), p. 124; *PP* 1846 VIII 292 (1971—4).

104. *PP* 1846 VIII 307 (2318) and 313 (2427).
105. *PP* 1846 VIII 467 (4359—60).
106. *PP* 1846 VIII 429 (3848).
107. *PP* 1846 VIII 357 (3197).
108. *Birmingham Advertiser*, 8 Oct 1846.
109. *Cheltenham Journal and Stroud Herald*, 6 Oct 1845 and 5 Oct 1846; *Hampshire Independent*, 4 Oct 1845, and *Hampshire Advertiser*, 26 Sep 1846; *Hertford Mercury and Reformer*, 29 Nov 1845, and *Hertfordshire County Press*, 12 Sep 1846.
110. M. Ostrogorski, *Democracy and the Organisation of Political Parties*, 2 vols (1902) vol. 1, p. lvii.
111. *The Times*, 4 July 1846.
112. Ibid., 8 July 1846.
113. *Hertford Mercury and Reformer*, 24 July 1847; *Worcestershire Guardian*, 12, 19 and 26 Dec 1846; *Worcestershire Chronicle*, 16 and 23 Dec 1846.
114. *Hampshire Independent*, 7 Aug 1847.
115. *Kentish Mercury*, 3 Aug 1847; *Maidstone Journal*, 27 July 1847.
116. *Hampshire Independent*, 7 Aug 1847; *Worcestershire Chronicle*, 9 Dec 1846; *Hertford Mercury and Reformer*, 7 Aug 1847.
117. *Essex Standard*, 13 Aug 1847.

CHAPTER 6

1. Eliot, the Chief Secretary, *PD* 3 ser. LXXIII 1692—1705, 1 Apr 1844.
2. *PD* 3 ser. LXXIII 1694—5 (Eliot) and 1716 (Peel), 1 Apr 1844.
3. *PD* 3 ser. LXXIII 1698, 1 Apr 1844 (Eliot), and LXXII 206—7, 2 Feb 1844 (Peel).
4. Eliot, *PD* 3 ser. LXXIII 1700, 1 Apr 1844.
5. Eliot, *PD* 3 ser. LXXIII 1699—1700, 1 Apr 1844.
6. *PD* 3 ser. LXXIII 1706 (M. O'Ferrall), 1710—11 (Lord John Russell), 1718—19 (French), and 1721 (M. J. O'Connell), 1 Apr 1844.
7. *PD* 3 ser. LXXV 145 (M. J. O'Connell), and 146—7 (Sheil), 1 July 1844.
8. Peel, *PD* 3 ser. LXXV 419—20, 10 June, and LXXVI 104—5, 28 June 1844.
9. *PP* 1847—8 LVII 210—11, and 1849 XLIX 465.
10. *PP* 1850 V 5—96.
11. *PD* 3 ser. CXII 756, 1 July (Desart), and 963—4, 5 July 1850 (Stanley).
12. Lord John Russell, *PD* 3 ser. CXIII 535—6, 30 July 1850.
13. *PP* 1851 L 879, 1852—3 LXXXIII 413, and 1860 LV 103.
14. Bright, *PD* 3 ser. CV 1196, 5 June 1849; J. A. Langford, *Modern Birmingham and its Institutions* vol. 2 (Birmingham, 1877) pp.

160—1.

15. *Correspondence between William Scholefield Esq. MP and Mr. J. B. Hebbert Respecting the Birmingham (Radical) Freehold Land Society and the Late Election for North Warwickshire* (Birmingham, 1852); 'First Report of the Commissioners Appointed to Inquire into Friendly and Benefit Building Societies', *PP* 1871 XXV 56 (3713).

16. E. J. Cleary, *The Building Society Movement* (1965) pp. 50—1.

17. Sir Harold Bellman, *Bricks and Mortals* (1949) p. 39.

18. W. W. Barry, *A Treatise on the Law and Practice of Benefit Building and Freehold Land Societies* (1866), p. 151.

19. *PD* 3 ser. CV 1207, 5 June 1849.

20. *Speeches . . . by Richard Cobden*, ed. Bright and Thorold Rogers, vol. 2, p. 494.

21. To Bright, 23 Dec 1848; quoted in J. Morley, *The Life of Richard Cobden* (1906) p. 503.

22. Morley, *Life of Cobden*, p. 521.

23. G. M. Trevelyan, *The Life of John Bright* (1913) p. 184.

24. F. E. Gillespie, *Labor and Politics in England 1850—1867* (Durham, N. Carolina, 1927), p. 95, note 1.

25. Cobden to James Taylor, *Warwick and Warwickshire Advertiser*, 7 Oct 1848.

26. *English Reports*, CXXXVI 1157—62.

27. *English Reports*, CXXXVIII 381—85.

28. H. F. A. Davis, *The Law of Building and Freehold Land Societies* (1870) pp. 310—11.

29. *English Reports*, CXLIII 871—4.

30. Morley, *Life of Cobden*, p. 501.

31. Ibid., p. 516; and Gillespie, *Labor and Politics 1850—1867*, pp. 80—105.

32. Trevelyan, *Life of Bright*, p. 185.

33. Cleary, *The Building Society Movement*, p. 52.

34. Bellman, *Bricks and Mortals*, pp. 46—7.

35. As Bright had feared; see Trevelyan, *Life of Bright*, pp. 185—6.

36. Cleary, *The Building Society Movement*, pp. 52—3.

37. See below, p. 129.

38. W. W. Barry, *Treatise*, p. 151.

39. R. G. Gammage, *History of the Chartist Movement 1837—1854* (Newcastle, 1894) pp. 192—3.

40. David J. V. Jones, *Chartism and the Chartists* (1975) pp. 90—1.

41. See Joy MacAskill, 'The Chartist Land Plan', in *Chartist Studies*, ed. A. Briggs (1959); and A. M. Hadfield, *The Chartist Land Company* (Newton Abbot, 1970).

42. Gammage, *History of the Chartist Movement*, pp. 194, 284—5.

43. For the development of party activity, see especially Ostrogorski, *Democracy and the Organisation of Political Parties* (1902); C. Seymour, *Electoral Reform in England and Wales* (New Haven, 1915); J. A. Thomas, 'Registration and the Development of Party Organisation 1832—1870', *History*, 1950; N. Gash, 'Peel and the

Party System', *Transactions of the Royal Historical Society*, 1951; and 'F. R. Bonham: Conservative "Political Secretary" 1832–47', *English Historical Review*, 1948; and C. O'Leary, *The Elimination of Corrupt Practices in British Elections 1868–1911* (Oxford, 1962).

44. Fraser, in *The New Poor Law in the Nineteenth Century*, pp. 111, 122–27.
45. Gammage, *History of the Chartist Movement*, Appendix B, pp. 411–26.
46. I am grateful to Professor Nichol Cooper for calling my attention to John Medway, *Memoirs of the Life and Writings of John Pye Smith* (1853) p. 384.
47. See above p. 44.
48. *PP* 1846 VIII 245 (917–921).
49. Seymour, *Electoral Reform*; Thomas, *Registration*; and H. J. Hanham, *Elections and Party Management* (1959) p. 399.
50. Select Committee on Registration of Voters (in the boroughs), *PP* 1868–9 VII 301–524; and Select Committee on Registration of Voters in Counties, *PP* 1870 VI 191–370.
51. 2 and 3 William IV c. 45, cl. xxx.
52. 14 and 15 Vict. c. 14.
53. *PD* 3 ser. CLXXXII 41 and 44, 12 Mar 1866.
54. See Hanham, *Elections and Party Management*, p. 401.
55. For the registration in Scotland, see especially John Cay, *An Analysis of the Scottish Reform Act, with the Decisions of the Courts of Appeal*, 2 parts (Edinburgh, 1837 and 1840); W. Ferguson, 'The Reform Act (Scotland) of 1832: Intention and Effect', *Scottish Historical Review*, 1966; *Papers on Scottish Electoral Politics 1832–1854*, ed. J. I. Brash (Edinburgh, 1974), which is excellent.
56. Select Committee on Registration of County Voters, *PP* 1864 X 403–604: the quotations are all from pp. 405–6.
57. 28 and 29 Vict. c. 36.
58. George Wilson, Secretary to the Anti-Corn Law League, *PP* 1846 VIII 416 (3650).
59. Uvedale Corbett, a revising barrister, *PP* 1860 XII 499 (3671).
60. H. Owen, clerk to the Poor Law Board, *PP* 1860 XII 506 (3733), and H. Smith, Conservative agent, *PP* 1864 X 455 (574).
61. *PP* 1884–5 XI 20 (234).
62. Prentice, *History of the Anti-Corn Law League*, vol. 2, p. 261.
63. *PP* 1852–3 LXXXIII 409.
64. *PP* 1857 (2) XXXIV 109.
65. *PP* 1866 LVII 47.
66. *PP* 1860 LV 85, 143, and 1862 XLIV 703. Statements of attitudes from Dod's *Parliamentary Companion*.
67. For Hume, Harvey, Yorke, Williams, Berkeley, Birch, Hall, Elphinstone, Laslett, Western, Locke King, and Blake, see Table 1. For Ayrton, see *PP* 1860 LV 109; Locke, *PP* 1860 LV 137; Bright, *PP* 1860 LV 39; Villiers, *PP* 1860 LV 189; Smith, *PP* 1859 XXIII 129; Collier, *PP* 1860 LV 119; Douglas, *PP* 1860 LV 1; White, *PP* 1864 XLVIII 237. Statements of attitudes from Dod's *Parliamentary*

Companion.

68. *PP* 1857–8 XLVI 571 and 1860 LV 109.
69. To Mrs Arbuthnot; quoted in Parker, *Sir Robert Peel*, vol. 2, p. 368.
70. Moore, *The Politics of Deference*.
71. Ibid., pp. 144–5.
72. For Professor Moore's treatment, see *The Politics of Deference*, chapter 4, section V.
73. Ibid., pp. 249, 273–5, 278–9.
74. Ibid., chapter 8; and, for the Reform Act, D. C. Moore 'Concession or Cure: The Sociological Premises of the First Reform Act', *Historical Journal*, 1966.

APPENDIX

1. T. E. May, *A Treatise upon the Law, Privileges, Proceedings and Usage of Parliament* (1844) p. 314.
2. For an account of the department's relations with its local officials, see A. P. Donajgrodski, 'The Home Office 1822–1848', D. Phil. thesis for Oxford University.
3. May, *Treatise*, pp. 314–15.
4. Lord Robert Montagu, *PP* 1860 LV 85.

Index

to text and to additional information
contained in the notes.

(I) is an entry relating to Ireland only.
N, S, E, W are divisions of counties.

Parish clerks, 35, 39
Parkes, J., 25, 28, 29, 39
Parliament, 3, 5, 6, 7, 10, 11, 12,
 24, 25, 27, 29, 38, 48, 49, 50,
 51, 58, 64, 78, 79, 95, 96,
 100, 105, 110, 122, 125, 130,
 133
Parliament, Acts of
 7 and 8 Wm. III c.25, 3, 89, 91,
  92, 93, 94, 111
 10 Anne c.23, 3
 18 Geo. II c.18, 3
 3 Geo. III c.15, 2
 20 Geo. III c.17, 4, 5
 28 Geo. III c.36, 4, 7, 8, 11, 21
 29 Geo. III c.13, 4, 11
 29 Geo. III c.18, 4, 11
 38 Geo. III c.60, 5
 39 and 40 Geo. III c.67, 51, 54,
  66, 70, 104
 42 Geo. III c.116, 5
 55 Geo. III c.26, 6, 62, 76, 78,
  84, 95, 96, 99, 102, 106, 110,
  111, 114, 121, 133
 9 Geo. IV c.59, 8
 10 Geo. IV c.8, 24, 51–2, 53, 54,
  55, 56, 57, 70, 71
 2 and 3 Wm. IV c.45, ch. 2, 23,
  25, 36, 39, 40, 43, 44, 46, 50,
  52, 62, 72, 74, 75, 79, 80, 81,
  82, 83, 88, 95, 112, 113, 118,
  119, 122, 124, 125, 128, 131,
  132, 133, 138, 141 n.3
 2 and 3 Wm. IV c.88, 53, 54, 55,
  56, 57, 59, 67, 68, 69, 70, 71,
  72
 4 and 5 Wm. IV c.76, 14–15
 5 and 6 Wm. IV c.76, 25, 39
 6 and 7 Wm. IV c.32, 108, 109,
  115, 123
 1 and 2 Vict. c.56, 104
 6 and 7 Vict. c.18, 72–7, 80,
  88–9, 120, 124, 131, 133
 7 and 8 Vict. c.32, 131
 10 and 11 Vict. c.90, 104
 11 and 12 Vict. c.90, 138
 13 and 14 Vict. c.69, 104–6
 14 and 15 Vict. c.14, 122
 28 and 29 Vict. c.36, 123

Parliament, Acts of (*cont.*)
 30 and 31 Vict. c.102, 122, 123,
  138
 8 Geo. V c.64, 125
Parliament, Bills of
 draft registration Bill of 1827, 7,
  8
 to establish register of borough
  voters, 1828, 8
 to register county voters, 1828, 8,
  9, 11
 registration Bill (I), 1835, 57, 61
 registration Bill, 1836, 48–9, 67
 registration Bill (I), 1836, 57, 59,
  61
 registration Bill (I), 1838, 59
 Stanley's registration Bill (I),
  1840, 60–6, 69, 71, 72
 franchise Bill (I), 1840, 66–7
 registration Bill (I), 1840, 66–7
 registration Bill, 1840, 66–7
 Stanley's registration Bill, (I),
  1841, 68
 Reform Bill (I), 1841, 68
 registration Bill, 1841, 68
 registration Bill, 1842, 72
 Factory Bill, 1843, 77
 registration Bill (I), 1844, 103–4
 Reform Bill, 1854, 125
 Reform Bill, 1859, 130
 Reform Bill, 1860, 125
 Reform Bill, 1866, 125
Parry, agent, 98
Party agents, 4, 16, 17, 22, 26, 28,
 29, 30, 34, 38, 39, 41, 50,
 56 (I), 61 (I), 73, 74, 78, 86,
 91, 92, 94, 95, 97, 98, 101,
 107, 118, 119, 120, 123, 130,
 133, 138
Party associations, 15, 23, 25, 98
Peel, Sir R., 23, 24, 26, 49, 50, 51,
 64, 68, 72, 75, 76, 77, 81, 82,
 83, 85, 87, 88, 90, 96, 97, 99,
 101, 102, 105, 107, 108, 110,
 115, 120, 121, 130, 131, 133
Peelites, 95, 100; *see also* Liberal
 Conservatives
Pennefather, R., Baron (I), 58, 105,
 145 n.56